Introducti

The Gower peninsula, lying to the w
'Area of Outstanding Natural Beauty' (
by 7¼ miles, this is a compact area that h
scenery, both along the coast and inland. Th
Reserves (Oxwich Bay, Gower Coast and Whiteford Burrows) as well as a large number of local reserves. Although generally low-lying, Gower has a number of areas of open access hill land and is the location of two long distance walking routes, the Gower Way and the Wales Coast Path.

Coastal scenery – beaches and cliff top paths – features strongly in this guide, with several of Gower's nature reserves being located on the coast. The coastline varies considerably, with rocky limestone cliffs, outcrops and small beaches to the south; the long sandy beaches of Rhossili and Whiteford to the west; the salt marshes and tidal flats of the Burry inlet and River Loughor to the north

The hills of the peninsula, as well as offering a range of great views, have prehistoric sites, wells, church and castle sites, as well as local nature reserves. Riverside and woodland walks lead into some of the more secluded parts of the area, taking in other nature reserves and passing historic and prehistoric features of interest. A number of walks centre around the Gower Heritage Centre at Parkmill, near the middle of the AONB.

The individual walks are mostly easy or moderate, with the majority fairly short, although many can be combined into longer routes. This guide can also be used as a basis for planning several linear routes, using buses. All walks are accessible by bus, with timetables available from Swansea's Quadrant Bus Station, Tourist Information Centres or online (www.traveline.cymru).

The use of walking boots and suitable clothing is recommended. Walkers are advised to check weather forecasts, the times of high tides if following beach routes and to check on-site safety notices. Exercise caution if you wish to detour to visit such places as Worm's Head, Burry Holms or the Old Lighthouse at Whiteford Point. The location of each walk is shown on the inside covers, together with approximate walking times and other information.

The first edition of this book was researched and written by Jane Griffiths; it has been a valuable guide to walking on the Gower. The present authors are grateful to Jane for the opportunity to update and add to her work. We hope that you enjoy the walks as much as we did.

WALK 1

OYSTERMOUTH & LIMESLADE BAY

DESCRIPTION This 4 mile walk starts near Oystermouth castle, a Norman fortification founded by William de Londres to keep a watchful eye over the Bay and Gower Peninsula. It dates principally from the 12th century, but with later additions. The walk is part urban and part coastal as it skirts Langland Bay and passes Limeslade Bay en route to Mumbles Hill with superb views across Swansea Bay which will soon witness the building of a majestic tidal lagoon.

START Oystermouth bus stop on Newton Road, SS 614882.

DIRECTIONS There's a regular daily bus service (nos. 2 & 2B) from Swansea Bus Station to Oystermouth/Newton. The Foreshore Car Park is near Newton Road.

1 *You may wish to look at the ruins of Oystermouth Castle across the road along Castle Avenue; there is an entrance charge. Then return to the bus stops.* Walk up the main street, Newton Road, rising to a crossroads then go LEFT into Langland Road. Cross over to enter the recreation ground and walk ahead, soon keeping left, across a road and by buildings, to a far left corner of Underhill Park to join a woodland path up steps to the road at Langland Corner. Cross with care; there are three roads off to the left in the direction of Langland Bay. Take the middle one, Rotherslade Road descending to the beach.

2 On reaching the promenade keep LEFT by a café, up steps to join the Wales Coast Path rising around the headland, then descending to Mumbles Road by a café left and Limeslade Bay right. Continue along the pavement; there's a restaurant, car park and Mumbles Head to the right. Just past this point cross the road and then take a path which cuts LEFT up the hillside and then bends RIGHT to climb more steeply up Mumbles Hill.

3 *This is a local nature reserve, mainly maritime heathland and limestone scrub with steep sided woodland stretching down to the Mumbles.* The path passes a mast to an interpretation board where there are great views across Swansea Bay. Continue along the path to pass by wartime gun platforms. Ignore paths off right, but instead keep ahead to a triangular patch of grassland. Continue towards the dwellings where you drop down to pass to the right of them.

4 Go RIGHT to descend Thistleboon Road and then RIGHT down Village Lane to reach Mumbles by many colourful houses. At the main road go LEFT to walk back down to the main junction with Newton Road in Oystermouth. Go LEFT into Newton Road where there is a bus stop for Swansea on the right.

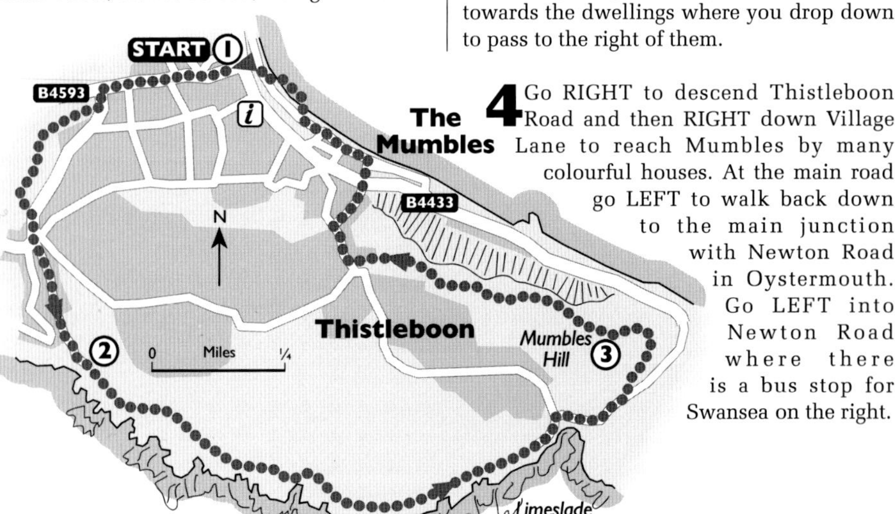

1 Cross the road from the bus stop to enter the car park; walk to the top end. From the information point at the rear of the car park go ahead for 25 yards, then LEFT up steps zig-zagging uphill and then RIGHT along the top edge of the wood until you reach a junction; go RIGHT to descend the hillside, slippy in places. Before reaching the bottom look for two fences. Go through the first gap and immediately turn LEFT up a sunken bridleway. Look for a narrow gap in a fence on the right with a path leading to St Peter's Chapel and Well. If not diverting to the chapel, stay on the main track as it rises out of the wood. At a junction by a gate on the left, turn RIGHT on a lane, Long Acre, in Murton.

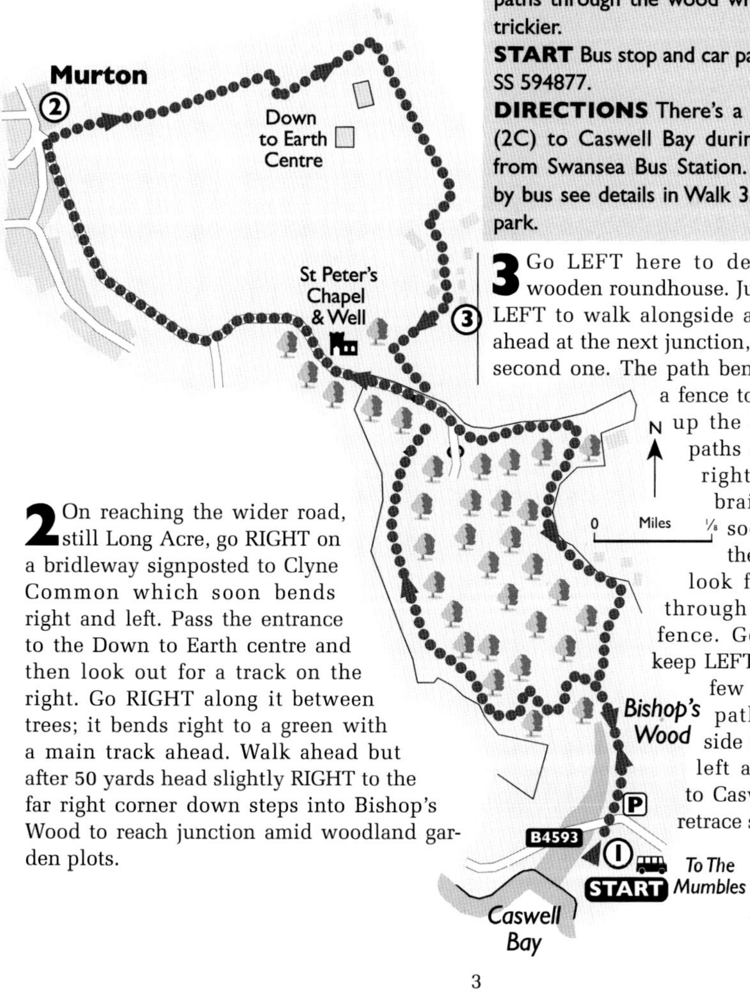

WALK 2

CASWELL BAY & BISHOPS WOOD

DESCRIPTION A moderate 2 mile walk starting at Caswell Bay passing through Bishop's Wood, limestone rich and ancient woodland, which is a Site of Special Scientific Interest. You will also pass by St Peter's Well and Chapel, now in ruins, and the Down to Earth education centre committed to eco-building, well-being and training. You return through new and ancient woodland; there are no stiles but paths can be muddy and there are many permissive paths through the wood which make navigation trickier.

START Bus stop and car park, Caswell Bay, SS 594877.

DIRECTIONS There's a regular bus service (2C) to Caswell Bay during summer months from Swansea Bus Station. For all year access by bus see details in Walk 3.There is a large car park.

2 On reaching the wider road, still Long Acre, go RIGHT on a bridleway signposted to Clyne Common which soon bends right and left. Pass the entrance to the Down to Earth centre and then look out for a track on the right. Go RIGHT along it between trees; it bends right to a green with a main track ahead. Walk ahead but after 50 yards head slightly RIGHT to the far right corner down steps into Bishop's Wood to reach junction amid woodland garden plots.

3 Go LEFT here to descend towards a wooden roundhouse. Just before this, turn LEFT to walk alongside a wire fence. Keep ahead at the next junction, then RIGHT at the second one. The path bends right alongside a fence to a junction. Climb up the hillside, ignoring paths off to the left and right; there are some braids too. You will soon see a house to the left; at this point look for a narrow path through a gap in a wire fence. Go through it and keep LEFT at a fork within a few yards. Follow the path down the hillside to the car park. Go left along a bridleway to Caswell Bay and then retrace steps.

WALK 3

CASWELL BAY & OYSTERMOUTH

DESCRIPTION A 4½ mile linear walk from Caswell Bay to Oystermouth following the Wales Coast Path to Langland and Limeslade bays with exceptional views across the Bristol Channel to Somerset and Devon.

START Bus stop at Caswell Drive, SS 599878. If arriving by car, park at Oystermouth Foreshore car park and catch the bus on Newton Road (see Walk 1).

FINISH Bus stop at Oystermouth Square, SS 615882

DIRECTIONS There's an hourly Monday-Saturday bus (2C) in the summer to Caswell Bay from Swansea Bus Station...start the walk at instruction 2. Otherwise, there is a 2/2A/3A, all year, to the end of Caswell Drive with a half mile walk to Caswell Bay.

2 Take the path off LEFT behind the cafés; this climbs up to Whiteshell Point and Newton Cliffs before descending for about half a mile into Langland Bay, passing by Langlands restaurants and the distinctive Edwardian beach huts before reaching the end of Rotherslade Road. This section is popular with dog walkers so please be watchful.

3 Rise up steps and climb again to Rams Tor on a surfaced path; there are great views from here across the Bristol Channel to Somerset. The path drops down and runs into a road alongside Limeslade Bay. Follow the Coast Path along the pavement to Bracelet Bay. You will see the coastguard station to the right and then further along the Mumbles lighthouse. As the main road swings left, keep ahead through a car park and drop down to Mumbles Pier, a superb reminder of our maritime heritage especially the lifeboat stations from different eras. Go LEFT to follow the sea front route by the older lifeboat houses and then onto the promenade to Oystermouth Square.

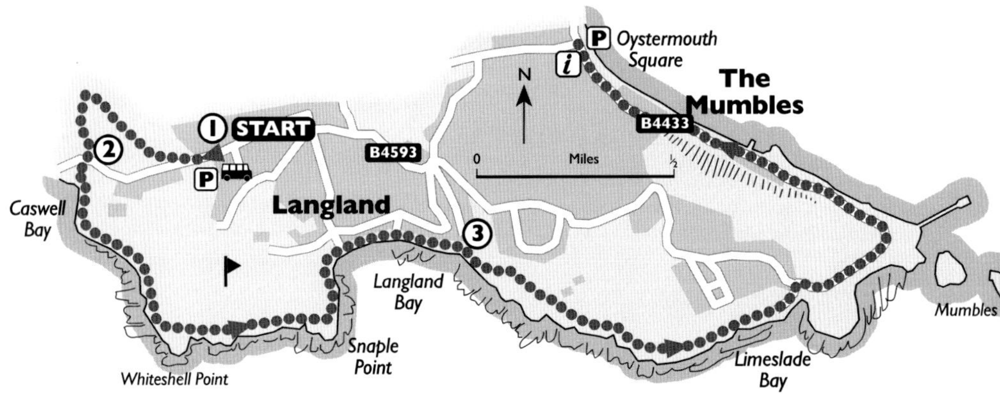

1 From the bus stop at Caswell Drive turn RIGHT to walk down for 100 yards to join a footpath RIGHT signposted to Bishopston. Follow this through woodland, past the Dingle garden to the right, and onward to a junction with a waymark. Continue ahead as the path descends to a junction. Go LEFT here through a gap in the fence and then zig zag down the hillside to the car park at Caswell. Cross the road to the bus shelter.

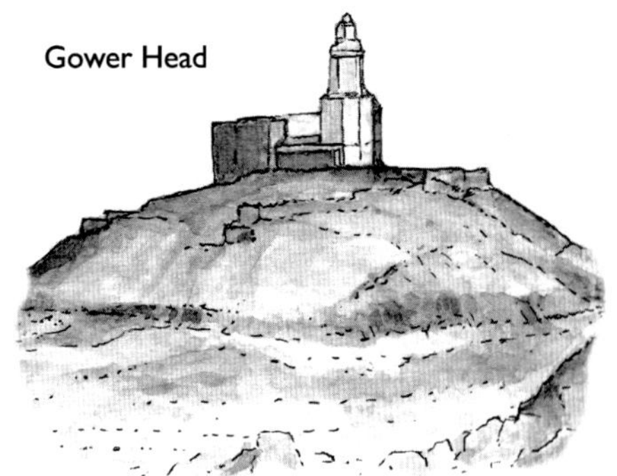

WALK 4
CASWELL BAY & PWLLDU BAY

DESCRIPTION A 4½ mile moderate walk from Caswell Bay to Brandy Cove, known to have been a smugglers' haunt in past times. The walk continues to the serene setting of Pwlldu Bay, a great place to rest awhile. Return via a headland, the Knap, and along a lane to Caswell and Caswell Bay; watch for traffic on the last bit. Do not attempt this walk at very high tides or in stormy weather!

START Caswell Bay, SS 594877.

DIRECTIONS There's an hourly Monday-Saturday bus (2C) in the summer to Caswell Bay from Swansea Bus Station. There is also a bus (2/2A/3A), all year, to the end of Caswell Drive, a half mile walk to Caswell Bay.... see walk 3, para 1. There's a substantial car park at the bay.

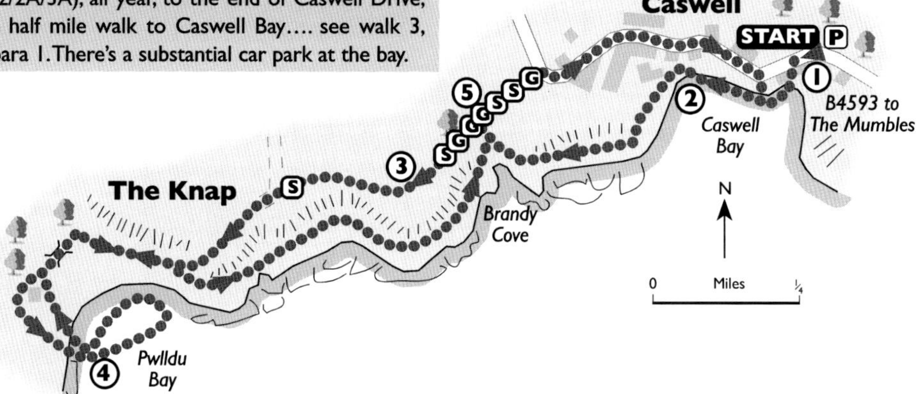

1 With your back to the bus stop at Caswell Bay turn LEFT to walk down to the beach and keep RIGHT along the edge of Caswell Bay beach. Pass the Lifeguard station and head HALF RIGHT to reach a path in the right hand corner.

2 Go up steep steps and at the junction go RIGHT on the coast path; it bends to the left and rises up to run along the coast to a junction of routes above Brandy Cove. From here you can cut LEFT to the cove. Otherwise, follow the path leading inland at a junction. Before reaching a barred gate, go through a kissing gate on the LEFT. Walk through a meadow to a second kissing gate and follow the path up steps through woodland to a stile which is crossed.

3 Continue ahead until you reach a waymark post before a bluff where you turn RIGHT. Follow the path along the hilltop; ignore the gate on the right. Cross a stile and go LEFT on a track descending to Pwlldu Bay, the view of the bay is exceptional. Cross a footbridge and follow the track around to the left past houses to the beach.

4 Retrace your steps back to the track and rise up the hillside, but look out for the Wales Coast Path sign where you turn RIGHT to follow the clear path back to the junction of paths above Brandy Cove.

5 At the junction, go LEFT up a track up the valley again. Proceed through the gate this time, but then turn RIGHT up steps. Go over a stile and follow the path along the right hand side of a field. Go over a stile by a gate and follow the track ahead to a kissing gate and a road. Turn RIGHT and follow the road back to Caswell Bay but watch for traffic as the road bends and some drivers seem to lack road awareness. When the road begins to dip down to Caswell Bay look for a path off to the right, just beyond Caswell Bay Court. Drop down steps to the beach to retrace your steps.

WALK 5

KITTLE & PWLLDU BAY

DESCRIPTION A 5½ mile energetic walk from Kittle to Bishopton Valley, much of which is in National Trust ownership. Some paths are uneven, stony and with climbs and steep descents; they can become muddy in places. The reward is a close look at caves, limestone sink holes and ancient woodland rich in wildlife. Pwlldu Bay is wonderfully quiet, but was not always so, for quarry workers, tinkers and woodlanders would converge on the hamlet to sup beer at hostelries which have long since gone. The return route to Kittle follows an old streambed past caves.

START Beaufort Arms, Kittle, SS 574893.

DIRECTIONS There's a regular bus (14) Monday-Saturday and a limited evening and Sunday service. On road parking near to the Beaufort Arms.

1 Start on the B4436 opposite the Beaufort Arms. Cross the green and follow the main track ahead, soon passing the National Trust plinth and bench to the left. On reaching Great Kittle farm leave the main track to join a path peeling off to the left of the buildings which leads into Bishopton Valley wood. The paths descends and then divides; take the RIGHT fork. Follow the path up steps and past an outcrop on the right, with a view across the valley. Now follow the path down steps and then back up more steps. Soon, the path descends again, steeply in places to reach a junction with a bridleway.

2 Turn RIGHT as signposted to Pwlldu following a bridleway with the stream to the left to a footbridge. Do not cross, but continue on the bridleway by the stream. On sighting a moss covered drystone wall keep to the left of it. On reaching open ground follow the track on the left hand side to reach a second footbridge. Once again, do not cross but continue ahead with the stream a little way to the left.

3 On reaching a three way waymark post, take the path leading LEFT. At the junction keep LEFT as the path zig-zags down to a junction by a stream. Go RIGHT as the path eases away from the stream to reach a National Trust waymark post. Drop down to a footbridge but do not cross it. Turn RIGHT to walk past the houses to Pwlldu Bay. Retrace your steps back to the footbridge but now cross it!

4 Follow the main track round to the right and uphill, ignoring the Coastal Path peeling off to the right. On reaching a stile, just off to the right, cross it and follow the path ahead, ignoring the gate off left. The path bends to the left and on reaching a waymark post go LEFT to descend to a stile. Cross it and drop down steps through a wood to a kissing gate. Once through, cross the pasture and pass through another kissing gate. Turn LEFT to a gate and track through the wood. Keep ahead and go through a gate near Hareslade farm.

5 Continue ahead on a track passing by the Swansea Community Tree Nursery Project. The track becomes a lane and you need to look out for a path on the LEFT. Follow this to proceed through a kissing gate, across a lane and along a drive, then passing to the right of the South Gower Rugby clubhouse. Go through a kissing gate, ahead again and through a second kissing gate and onward to go through a gap at the end of the field. Proceed through a kissing gate onto a lane. Turn RIGHT and follow it to a point where the lane bends gently right. Go LEFT here on a track. When it meets a concrete surface go through a kissing gate to the LEFT.

6 Follow the path through another kissing gate and descend old stone steps to pass by a National Trust plinth at Bishopston Valley. At a marker post go ahead on the centre path into the valley. Cross a footbridge and turn RIGHT following the sign for Kittle/ Bishopston. At the next waymark post continue towards Bishopston. At a fork in the path go RIGHT and cross an old streambed. Head LEFT soon reaching another waymark post.

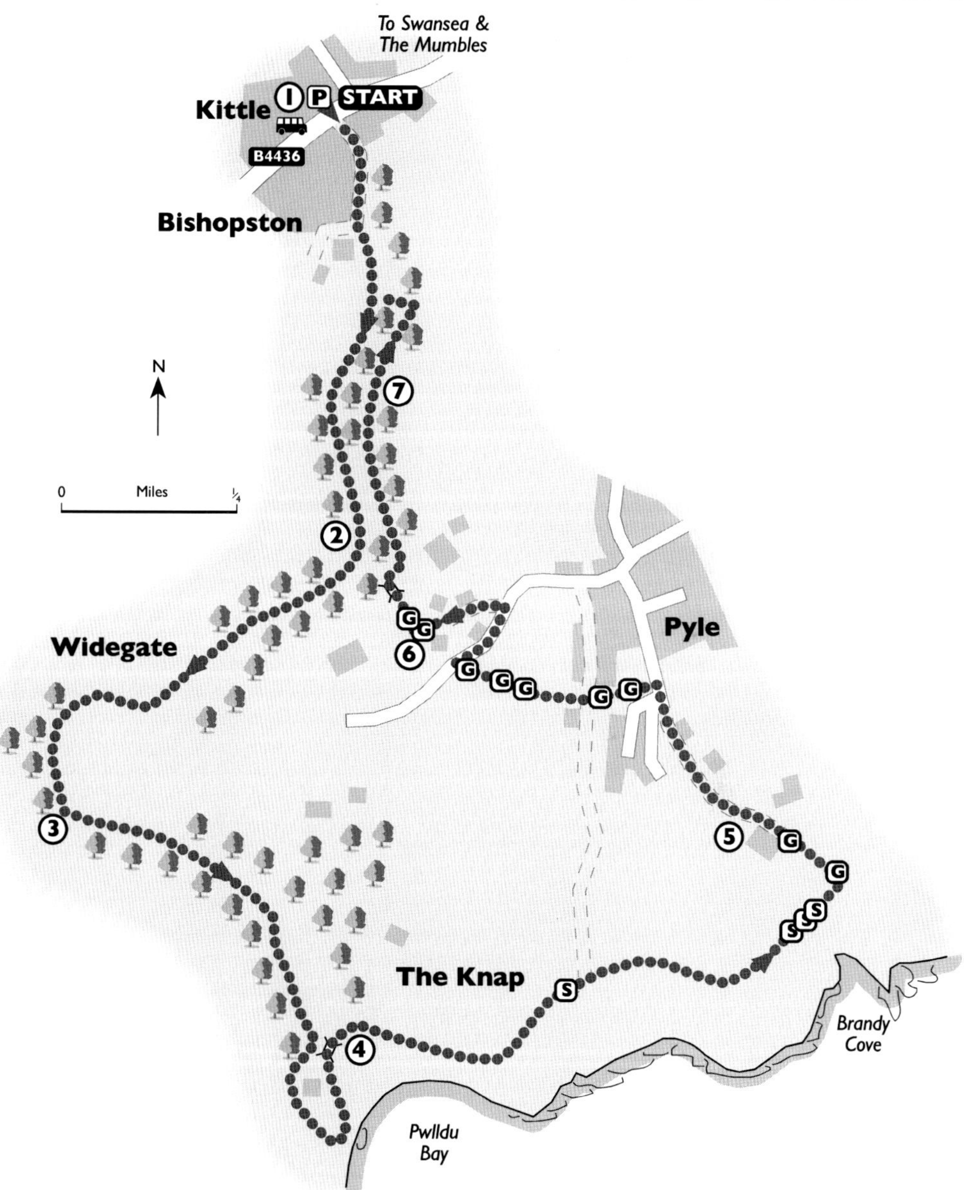

7 Pass by an entrance to a small cave and then an outcrop. Continue along a stony path now following an old streambed; there's a second cave off to the left. On sighting a waymark post on the left cross the old streambed and follow the path up steps towards Kittle. Pass a third cave on the left and on reaching the junction turn RIGHT. Follow the path back past Great Kittle Farm and continue ahead to the village green and Beaufort Arms.

WALK 6

PENNARD CLIFFS & PWLLDU BAY

DESCRIPTION This 4½ mile moderate walk starts at the roundabout at Pennard Cliffs. It follows the Wales Coast Path across headlands to Pwlldu Bay with fine views out to sea on this quieter stretch, then returning through farmland and the ancient woodlands, Bishopston and Lockway Woods, to venture back to Pennard Cliffs where toilets, café and shops are available.
START Pennard Cliffs car park and bus stop, SS 554874.
DIRECTIONS There's a regular bus (14) Monday-Saturday from Swansea Bus Station and a limited evening and Sunday service. Car parking at National Trust car park, East Cliff.

1 From the bus stop head seawards towards the end of the National Trust car park. Turn LEFT to join the Wales Coast Path following a path parallel to a road on your left as far as Hunt's farm.

2 Beyond the farm turn slightly RIGHT as waymarked to climb up to Pwlldu Head where there are excellent views across to Caswell Bay. Follow the footpath downhill, ahead at first then LEFT to climb back up again to reach a gate onto farmland. Go through the gate and follow the path running to the right of the fence. Go through a second gate and head across the field to a further gate. Follow the path through a mixture of scrub and woodland through another kissing gate to the right of houses to a barred gate. Continue ahead for a few yards to a track.

3 Turn RIGHT at the junction and follow the track downhill. On nearing a gate leading to a house turn sharp RIGHT onto a bridleway to descend a sunken lane down to Pwlldu. At a junction at the bottom, turn RIGHT and pass by houses to join a track at Bishopston Pill.

4 Turn LEFT and follow the track back to the houses. Retrace your steps back up the sunken lane to the junction at the track where you walked previously. Cross it and follow the footpath to climb a stile. Continue down the footpath alongside the boundary fence to a second stile. Cross it and continue ahead on a path through a meadow keeping to the right hand side of the field. Follow a green lane to a stile into the next field.

5 Proceed ahead alongside Bishopston Wood and when the path dips look out for a stile on the right to enter the wood. Ignore the path off left alongside the fence. Your way is ahead into the woodland, passing the remains of an old stile and steps. Follow the path downhill and to the left; continue along the path to reach a junction where there is a waymark.

6 Take the path leading ahead, signposted for Kittle and Bishopston. Follow it alongside Bishopston Pill to a fork in the route. Turn LEFT here at the waymark post signposted Southgate. Follow the track up the valley through Lockway Wood. Pass through a gap to the left of a gate and very soon take the LEFT fork, signposted for Southgate.

7 At the end of the wood, continue ahead on an enclosed track, ignoring a footpath leading off to the right. Pass through a gate and continue ahead past a house known as

Hael. Follow the access track as it bends left and right through a gate and then ahead. At the junction of tracks, by bungalows, turn LEFT. Follow the track/lane back to the car park/bus stop/café for welcome refreshment.

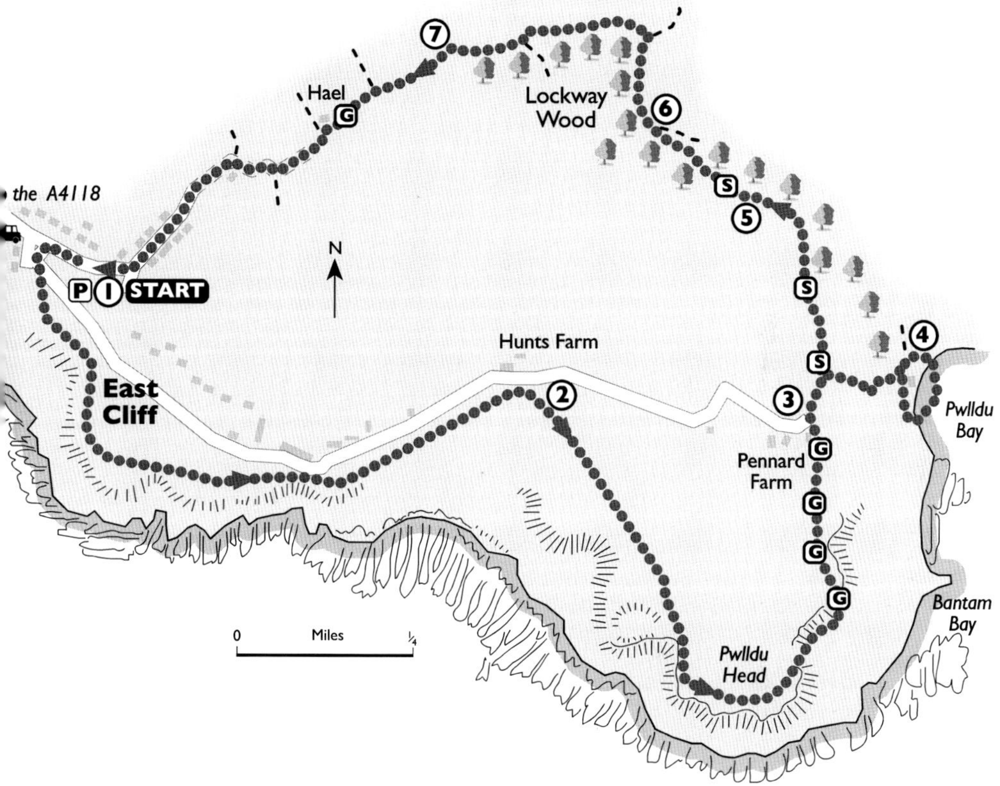

the A4118

P I START

N

Hael

G

7

Lockway Wood

6

S

5

S

S

4

Hunts Farm

East Cliff

2

3

Pwlldu Bay

Pennard Farm

G

G

G

G

Bantam Bay

0 Miles ¼

Pwlldu Head

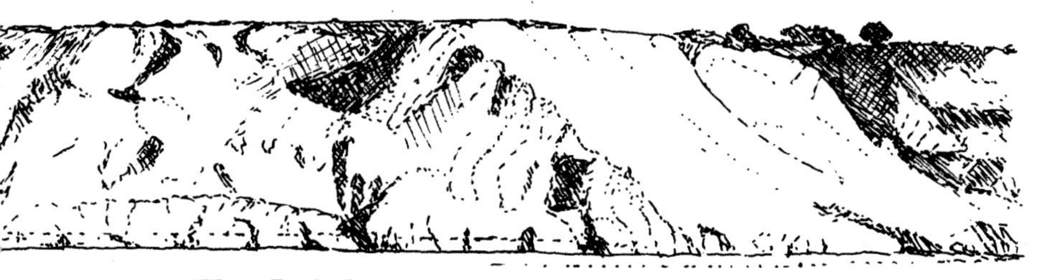

Pwlldu Head

WALK 7

PENNARD (WEST CLIFF) & PARKMILL

DESCRIPTION A 5 mile moderate walk from Pennard (West Cliff) to Parkmill by way of Southgate and the haunting ruins of Pennard Castle, returning on the coastal path along West Cliff where there's a café and shop. There are some climbs and sandy sections; the views across Three Cliffs Bay are exceptional

START Pennard Cliffs car park and bus stop, SS 554874.

DIRECTIONS There's a regular bus (14) Monday-Saturday and a limited evening and Sunday service. National Trust Car Park.

1 Start at the bus stop by the Three Cliffs Coffee Shop. Walk around the turning circle to take the far road, Southgate Road. This bends LEFT and soon passes by a bungalow on the left to cross a stile into a field. Go LEFT, cross a stile into woodland and proceed ahead. Exit over a stile and keep RIGHT in a field following a hedge to cross a stile by a gate. Go ahead again to cross a stile. Follow a corralled path by a school, keeping RIGHT at a junction through a gate to Pennard Road.

2 Cross it to join a waymark post and then head slightly right, parallel to the track along the edge of a golf course; there waymarks for most of the way but they peter out at a sandy patch. Cut right to walk down the RIGHT fork of the track, Sandy Lane. On reaching another track, Norton Drive, go RIGHT to walk by houses. At a junction continue ahead down a track which bends left. Go LEFT on a footpath opposite an old garage to descend through woodland to pass houses. Go LEFT onto a track and rise up to a road.

3 Cross the road to join another woodland path which eventually descends to a junction by a footbridge. Cut right here if you wish to visit the Gower Heritage Centre; cross the road with care. Without the detour, follow the path up to a junction; go LEFT to climb up to houses as signposted to Southgate. Keep ahead behind houses then across the golf course; aim for the ruins of Pennard Castle, dating originally from the 12th century through to the 14th century. The views across to Three Cliffs Bay are magnificent.

4 From here the path dips slightly left of the ruins; it is less clear as the shifting sands make instructions less easy. Head slightly RIGHT down the main track. Cross this and keep climbing slightly RIGHT to the headland until you reach one of the waymarks guiding you ahead on the Wales Coast Path. There are steps and the path bends left and right before descending to a gully and a cross track down to Pobbles beach.

5 Continue ahead across the track, go LEFT and RIGHT to climb once again, keeping LEFT at the top and ahead through gorse bushes. Continue ahead on a wide green way and then on a lane, West Cliff, back to the starting point.

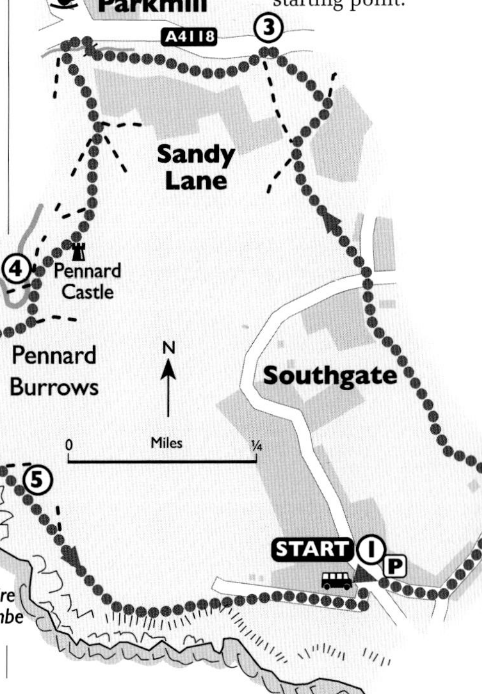

WALK 8

PARC-LE-BREOS WOODLANDS

DESCRIPTION This is an easy 4 mile walk, which starts along an attractive wide grassy valley with woods on each side and containing a restored Neolithic burial chamber and also the entrance to a cave used as a bronze age burial site. The walk continues through restful shady woodland to reach the edge of open land near Cefn Bryn ridge, and returns to the start along a gentle route through pasture and woods. Refreshments are available at the Gower Heritage Centre.

START Shepherds Store, Parkmill, SS 545892.

DIRECTIONS The 118 bus (Monday – Saturday) and the 118/114 Gower Explorer (Summer Sundays) between Swansea and Rhossili call at Parkmill; alight at the stop for the Gower Heritage Centre. If coming by car, park at the Heritage Centre, which is a short distance from the bus stop; alternatively park at the small Forestry Commission car park (SS 538896) at the end of Section 1 below.

1 From the bus stop take the lane past Shepherds store which then passes houses to reach the Heritage Centre; just after the entrance cross a footbridge to the right of a ford and turn RIGHT on the lane. In a few minutes you will reach a car parking area on your left.

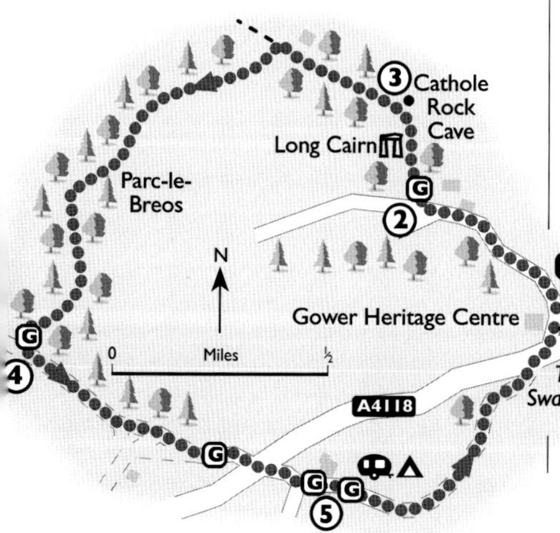

2 Turn RIGHT through a kissing gate, passing an information board. Follow the track along the valley towards the burial chamber, which is to the left of the track. Now cross to the right hand side of the valley, pass a lime kiln and look for an information board about Cathole Cave. Turn RIGHT up past this into the wood and you will soon see on your right a gate barring a minor entrance to the cave. Turn RIGHT past this gate to reach a much larger (also barred) entrance on the left.

3 Return to the valley and turn RIGHT. When you reach a junction of tracks with a house visible to the right, turn LEFT. Follow the stony track through the woods, ignoring side turnings. Eventually the track (now a path) bends to the left to reach a kissing gate. Go through this and turn LEFT on a track.

4 Stay on the main track as it gradually descends. When it ends, join a lane and follow this down through a kissing gate next to a cattle grid to reach a junction with Penmaen Church on your right. Cross the main road with care and continue down the lane opposite. At the next junction ignore the right turn and keep ahead, signed to the Holiday Park. Go through the gate at the end of the yellow lines (bridleway sign nearby on left).

5 Walk ahead between the buildings and continue in the same direction along a lane and then enclosed track. The track eventually descends into woodland and reaches the main road. Cross over carefully and walk along the lane towards the Heritage Centre. Bear RIGHT across the footbridge and return to the bus stop/car park. (If you parked at the Forestry Commission car park, don't cross the footbridge; instead bear LEFT just before the ford and go up the lane to the car park.)

WALK 9

ILSTON CWM & ELIZABETH & ROWE HARDING NATURE RESERVE

DESCRIPTION This is a memorable (moderate) inland walk of about 5 miles. It includes several stretches of beautiful woodland, a ruin with considerable historical interest on the site of a pre-reformation chapel, a church dating from the 13th C and a very remarkable nature reserve on the site of an old quarry. Towards the end of the walk, it goes down an ancient Cwm (valley) of moss-covered trees (and bluebells in Spring). Refreshments are available at the Gower Heritage Centre, and also at the Gower Inn (section 2 below). (To make a longer walk of about 9 miles, when you get to the kissing gate towards the end of section 7, don't go through it. Instead turn RIGHT to pick up walk 8 (page 11) at the start of section 2.)

START Shepherds Store, Parkmill, SS 545892.

DIRECTIONS The 118 bus (Monday – Saturday) and the 118/114 Gower Explorer (Summer Sundays) between Swansea and Rhossili call at Shepherds Store, Parkmill; alight at the stop for the Gower Heritage Centre. If coming by car, park at the Heritage Centre, which is a short distance from the bus stop; from the entrance to the Centre don't cross the stream but walk back past houses to the main road (A4118).

1 Cross over carefully and follow the road to the LEFT for a very short distance then, immediately after Maes-yr-Haf, turn RIGHT on a path over a footbridge. Head up the steps on the LEFT and follow the path through woodland up two more sets of steps. Then keep to the main lower path near the fence on the left; this leads to a junction with a lane.

2 Cross over and continue down a stony track to turn LEFT over a footbridge to the main road. Cross over and walk carefully (no footpath) along a short stretch of road past an outdoor activity centre. Just before reaching the Gower Inn, turn LEFT on a way-marked footpath that runs just to the left of the pub car park. On reaching the end of the car park bear slightly RIGHT on a path that leads across an open area and back into trees. Cross a footbridge and continue ahead.

3 Cross a second footbridge; just after this in a magical setting on the right can be seen the remains of Trinity Well Chapel – *with a plaque commemorating the foundation of the first Baptist church in Wales at Ilston in 1649.* After looking at the ruins, return to the path. Keep ahead (ignoring a left fork along the river). Quite soon turn RIGHT at a junction to walk just to the right of the river; depending on weather conditions the river can vary from being completely dry to having a vigorous flow of water. Keep on the main path over 4 bridges, crossing and re-crossing the river, until finally the river is on your left.

4 At a T junction bear LEFT. Cross a very small bridge and eventually reach a gate leading into the churchyard. *The church, which dates from the 13thC, is worth a visit (if open), especially for the bells.* Continue ahead to exit the churchyard through a gate; then cross (yet another!) footbridge to reach the road. Turn RIGHT to walk through the village past houses.

5 Look for a ford on the left, leading to a stile into the Elizabeth and Rowe Harding Nature Reserve, owned by the Wildlife Trust of South and West Wales; *Rowe Harding was a notable Welsh Rugby player, and he and his wife donated sections of the land to the Wildlife Trust. The reserve is the site of an old limestone quarry, and has a dramatic vertical rock face which is a Geological SSSI because of its very unusual layered rock structure. The area in front of the rock face has an abundance of wild flowers in summer, and there is also some attractive woodland.* Turn sharp left to cross the ford if possible – *but **look carefully** at the flow of water before doing so. **If the river is overflowing from its narrow channel, trying to cross it can***

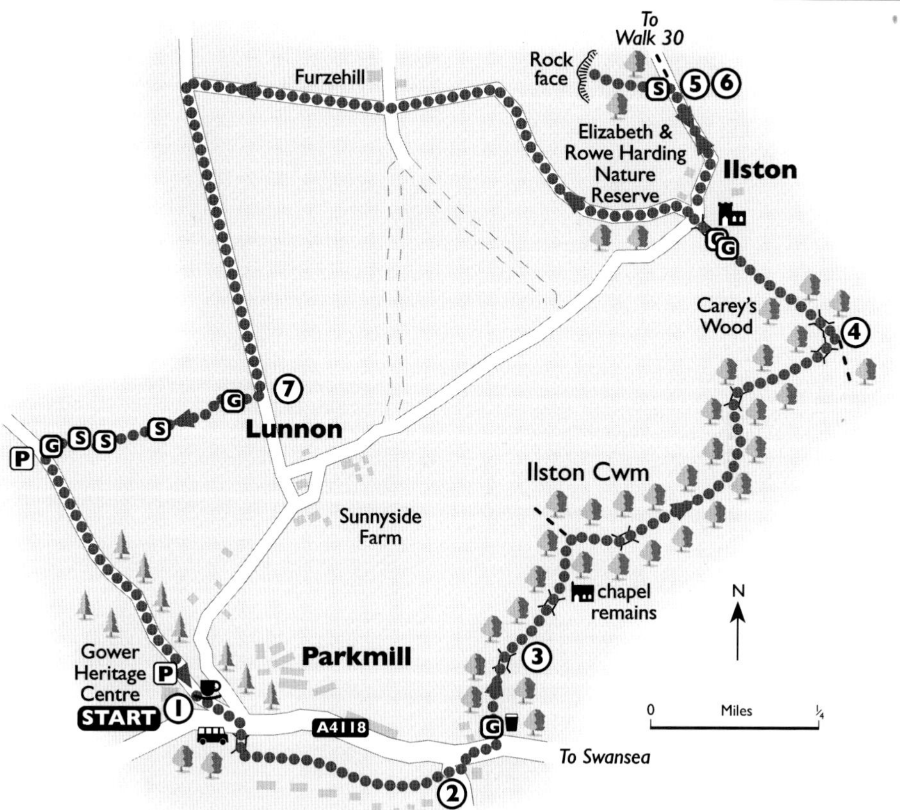

be dangerous. If in doubt, return towards the village, cross the road bridge over the river and immediately turn RIGHT along the drive leading to Underwood; the gate into the reserve is on the right. Then keep near the right hand side of the reserve and you will find the gate and stile next to the ford. If coming over the stile, take the wide track up and round to the right, and before long reach the rock face and interpretation board on the left. ***Do not approach too close to the rock face.*** There are also other paths which can be explored.

6 On leaving the reserve, walk back into the village; just before the Council notice-board on the left, turn RIGHT along a narrow road. (If you get back to the church, you've gone too far.) Follow this little used road uphill (with the reserve on your right). The road bends to the left next to a turning for Bryn-afel. Continue on the road past another turning on the right, and before long reach a junction. Turn LEFT. Take care on the next stretch, as vehicles sometimes travel at speed. Just after the 30 mph sign, turn RIGHT down the drive towards Ashgrove.

7 Go through the gate to the right of the garage and then on down the path, which wends its way through Willoxton Cwm, over a stile into an open wilderness. Soon the path crosses another stile to go up and down steps next to the fencing of a Welsh Water treatment works (apparently disused) and then to emerge over a final stile onto a large grassy area. Bear LEFT to a kissing gate; once through this, turn LEFT down the road to the Heritage Centre. Turn LEFT to cross a bridge over a stream, pass the Heritage Centre and continue down the road to reach the bus stop on the main road.

WALK 10

CEFN BRYN & ARTHUR'S STONE

DESCRIPTION This is a moderate 6½ mile walk along a sandstone ridge, often referred to as the backbone of Gower. The ridge reaches the second highest point on the Gower peninsula (186m) (Rhossili Down is higher by 7 metres) and gives splendid views on both sides. The walk also visits a prehistoric burial chamber with a 25 ton capstone, which has been an attraction for hundreds of years; Henry VII's troops are said to have made a 128 km detour to visit the stone before the battle of Bosworth Field in 1485.

START Penmaen Church, SS 532887.

DIRECTIONS The 118 bus (Monday – Saturday) and the 118/114 Gower Explorer (Summer Sundays) between Swansea and Rhossili call at Penmaen Church. For car parking, turn right at the church, if coming from Swansea. There is a parking area just over the cattle grid on the right, and a small car park with picnic benches a little further up the lane on the left.

1 Walk up the lane with the church on your left. Cross a cattle grid and continue on the lane round to the left. Soon you pass the Three Cliffs Care Home on your left.

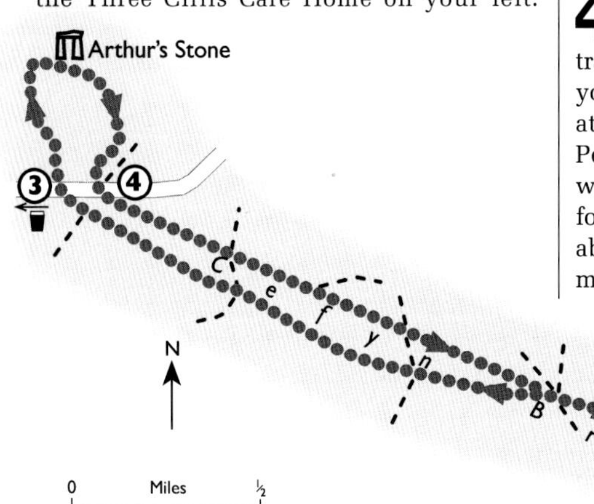

Immediately after this, but before reaching The Old Post (a house), fork RIGHT up a stony track. At a junction of tracks with a Gower Way plinth on the right, fork LEFT, now joining the Gower Way.

2 When you reach a large boulder on the left, fork LEFT immediately after the boulder on a grassy track. This will enable you to read the inscription plate about the Gower Way which is on the back of the boulder. Follow the track round the curve of the hill, soon rejoining the other track. Continue gently uphill to pass a building, a fenced area and a trig point on the right. At a Gower Way plinth (no. 11) fork LEFT, and continue ahead along the ridge for some time, until you see a toposcope on the right. Soon after this the track reaches a road. *(If you need refreshment by now, you can turn left down the road to Reynoldston; continue ahead at a cross-roads to reach the King Arthur Hotel, about ½ mile from the ridge. But you will have to walk back up the hill afterwards!)*

3 Cross the road. Don't take the bridleway to your left, but go along a grassy track at right angles to the road. The top of the capstone is just visible ahead peeping over the bracken. When you get to Arthur's Stone, follow a grassy track curving round to the RIGHT back to the road, a little way downhill from where you turned off. Cross over.

4 Do not follow the waymarked footpath but instead turn LEFT along a grassy track; keep going in the same direction until you reach the junction with the Gower Way at plinth 11. Keep left uphill, returning to Penmaen by the route you came on. If you want a more varied, but longer, route back, follow stage 7 (B) of walk 29 – this will take about ½ hour longer than the direct route, more if you stop at the farm for refreshments!

WALK 11

PENMAEN BURROWS

DESCRIPTION This 3½ mile walk is moderate on the whole, though it involves a steep climb up a sandy path which can be quite hard work. It's worth the effort, though, as it leads to a beautiful circuit around Penmaen Burrows, with great views, and with the added interest of ancient remains of a buried medieval church, a Neolithic burial chamber and the earthworks of a Norman castle. Refreshments are available at the Gower Heritage Centre.

START Shepherds Store, Parkmill, SS 545892.

DIRECTIONS The 118 bus (Monday – Saturday) and the 118/114 Gower Explorer (Summer Sundays) between Swansea and Rhossili call at Parkmill; alight at the stop for the Gower Heritage Centre. If coming by car, park at the Heritage Centre.

1 From the bus stop take the lane past Shepherds which then passes houses to reach the Heritage Centre; just after the entrance cross a footbridge to the right of a ford and turn LEFT on the lane to reach the main road. (This route is much safer than walking along the main road from the bus stop.) Cross over with care, turn RIGHT and almost at once bear LEFT along a bridle way. Follow this uphill. The track eventually passes through a gate and reaches a farm/camp site.

2 Take the left hand gate and follow the lane to a T junction. Turn LEFT. Soon you reach a National Trust sign. Bear LEFT just in front of this up to a small secluded area of recovering heathland. Pass a right turn and at the second junction of paths bear RIGHT to reach a viewpoint and bench. Return to the junction, bear LEFT and soon turn LEFT. The path goes down steps to a lane.

3 Turn LEFT and follow the lane for a short way to a waymarked path on the RIGHT. Go down this path, keeping RIGHT at a junction to join the Coast Path, and cross a footbridge at the bottom. Turn RIGHT up a steep sandy path to the top of Penmaen Burrows. Turn RIGHT (signed to Penmaen). In a few minutes you will see an opening going slightly uphill on the right – *in this are the buried remains of a medieval church, covered by the sand in the 14thC.* On the other side of the path, just before you get to the church, is a narrow path which leads in ½ minute or so to a small low burial chamber on your right.

4 Continue on the path towards Penmaen, and in a few more minutes, just before a gate in front, turn LEFT along a bridleway. At the next junction (with a view of a double limekiln to the right), turn LEFT. Keep RIGHT at the next three junctions to follow the path round the cliff top. As the path bends left away from the sea, you will see a path leading through a large bank on your right. This is the site of an old Norman castle, and if you walk through the gap you can see the large ditch around you. Go back to the path, and on completing the circuit of the Burrows, turn RIGHT down the path you came up on, cross the footbridge and follow the path up to the lane. Turn LEFT and continue up to the T junction. Here turn RIGHT back to the start.

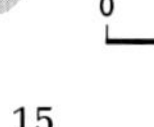

9/2/18.

WALK 12

NICHOLASTON BURROWS, BEACH & WOODS

DESCRIPTION This is a moderate 3 mile walk which includes some of coastal Gower's most beautiful features, cliffs, woods, dunes and beaches, yet which is relatively secluded. In summer there is an amazing variety of flowers (including pyramidal orchids) to be seen on leaving woodland in Section 2. The walk can easily be extended to 6 miles by crossing the footbridge at the end of Section 2 to join walk 13.

START Penmaen House Bus Stop, SS 526885. (This is the stop after Penmaen Church, coming from Swansea.)

DIRECTIONS The 118 bus (Monday – Saturday) and the 118/114 Gower Explorer (Summer Sundays) between Swansea and Rhossili call at Penmaen. There is a small car park next to the bus stop, or turn up off the main road over a cattle grid by the bus stops to find a parking area on your left.

1 From the bus stop on the seaward side of the road, go through a waymarked gate at the lower end of the parking area and continue ahead. After a while pass through another gate (National Trust sign for Penmaen Burrows). Take the next turning on the RIGHT. Turn RIGHT at a junction to go past a double limekiln and, before long, go through a gate. On reaching a waymark post, continue ahead (signed for Coast Path and Nicholaston).

2 Ignore turnings to left and right. The path descends steeply down a sandy stretch to a junction by a large tree. Turn RIGHT and then, at the next junction, LEFT down steps. Keep RIGHT down the Coast Path just past a notice board for Oxwich Bay. This path emerges from the woods at Nicholaston Burrows. Head across the dunes on one of the paths leading to the beach. Turn RIGHT and follow the beach until nearing the point where a stream runs out into the sea. Bear RIGHT to follow the stream to a footbridge.

3 Do not cross the bridge but turn RIGHT along a sandy path. Continue, passing a number of waymark posts, as the path approaches and then goes next to the wooded slopes on your left. Follow the waymarked route back into woodland and then out again at the place where you came out of the wood earlier. *(If you feel in need of refreshment by now, retrace your earlier route back up into the wood, past the Oxwich Bay notice board and up the steps. Then turn LEFT along a path which will soon bring you to a stone stile leading to Nicholaston Farm and its café (summer only). Afterwards return to the wood to pick up the homeward route.)* Walk straight on across dunes and to your left you will see a number of sandy paths going up into the woods. The first one of these will take you back to the noticeboard, but others go up through the woods; turn LEFT up one of these, and at the top turn RIGHT to rejoin the path you came out on.

4 When you reach the waymark post passed earlier, turn LEFT (signed to Penmaen) to go through a gate, then after a while another gate. Turn LEFT. Go through another gate, and turn LEFT to rejoin the track you came on originally. Soon a final gate leads to the main road. To get to the bus stop for Swansea, cross the road with care and turn RIGHT; the bus stop is just after the junction.

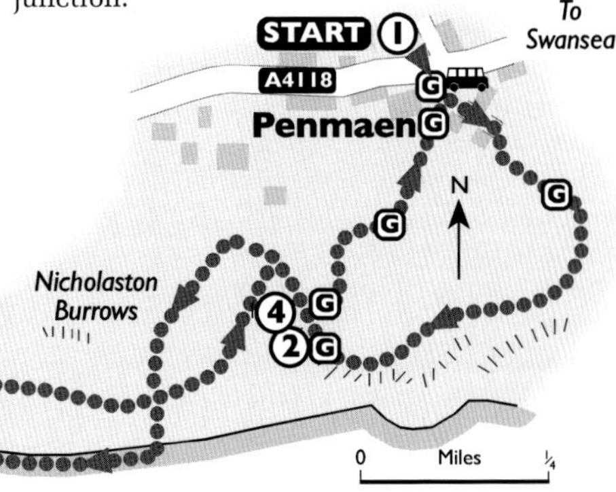

WALK 13

OXWICH BURROWS & BEACH

DESCRIPTION An easy 3 mile walk through the dunes at Oxwich Burrows, part of the National Nature Reserve which is a must for lovers of plant life. In particular, there are several varieties of orchids and birds such as warblers and bittern to be seen. It is sheltered from the prevailing south westerly winds and tides by Oxwich headland and whilst the dunes have been stable for centuries they now suffer from trampling by people. By far the best time to visit is early summer when the orchids are in bloom. The return is along one of the loveliest beaches on the Gower Peninsula.

START Oxwich Beach Car Park, Oxwich Bay, and nearby bus stop, SS 501865.

DIRECTIONS There's a daily bus in summer and Mondays to Saturdays in winter (118 connecting to 117). The bus stop is next to the car park

1 Mid-way along from the entrance to the eastern edge of the car park take the path into the burrows. Within a few steps turn LEFT at the fork to walk through thick foliage; the path runs parallel to the road and bends slightly right. Ignore a stile on the left leading to the road and continue to follow the path to a kissing gate. Continue along the path until you reach a junction with a sandy track.

2 The path now veers slightly RIGHT easing gently between a pocket of woodland below and rising dunes to the right. This is the Wales Coast Path and you are guided through areas festooned with wild flowers which are delightful when in full bloom during the summer months. Please keep to the path to avoid damage to the dunes. Follow the waymarks to reach a bridge over the water channel. The path ahead leads to Nicholaston Burrows, Beach and Woods walk.

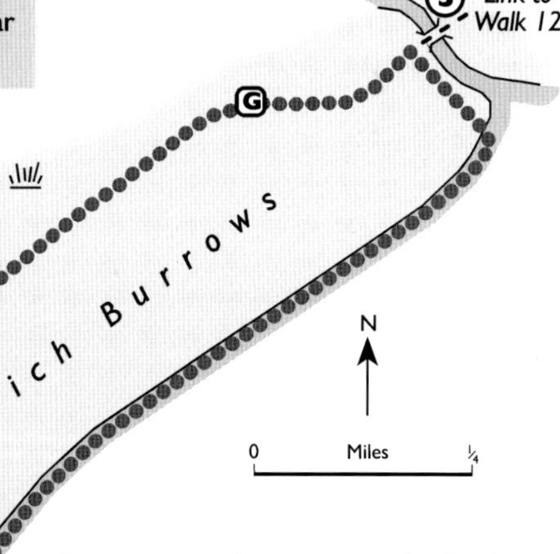

3 However, do not cross the bridge. Turn RIGHT to follow the water channel, Nicholaston Pill, towards Oxwich Beach. There are fine views across to the cliffs on the left. Turn RIGHT to walk along the beach back to the cafés, restaurant, toilets and car park/bus stop. It is tempting to take your boots or trainers off to dabble your toes in the water even if the weather isn't scorching hot that day!

WALK 14

OXWICH HEADLAND

DESCRIPTION An energetic 5 mile walk around Oxwich headland offers exceptional views out to sea. There is a steep climb out of Oxwich, but otherwise the walk is moderate. You pass St Illtyd's church, coastal woodland and limestone cliffs on this first part. There is a chance to detour to a rocky inlet, The Sands, before returning inland to Oxwich, Oxwich Castle and the beach.
START Oxwich Bay car park and adjacent bus stop, SS 501865.
DIRECTIONS There's a daily bus in summer and Mondays to Saturdays in winter (118 connecting to 117). The bus stop is next to the car park at Oxwich Cross.

1 Start at the bus stop by the car park. Turn LEFT to walk to the crossroads. Go LEFT again and follow the No Through lane to the end. Continue ahead on a tarmac and then unsurfaced track to St Illtyd's church, origins from the 6th century, but the present church was built mainly in the 12th and 14th centuries. The path runs to the left of the church and then bears RIGHT to climb over one hundred steps.

2 On reaching a junction turn LEFT as signposted on the Wales Coast Path to Oxwich Point. Follow this main path through the woods and by a field. Continue ahead and then drop down nearer to the sea's edge. The path bends RIGHT and ahead to eventually exit the woodland. Continue ahead to go through a kissing gate.

3 Follow the path ahead and take the LEFT fork at a waymark post, following the sign for the Coast Path and Horton. The path rounds Oxwich Point with good views of Port Eynon Bay. At the next waymark post continue to follow the Coast Path as signposted to Horton. Go through two kissing gates and then the path keeps company with a fence on your right. Pass through a kissing gate, soon after which the small bay, The Sands, can be seen to the left.

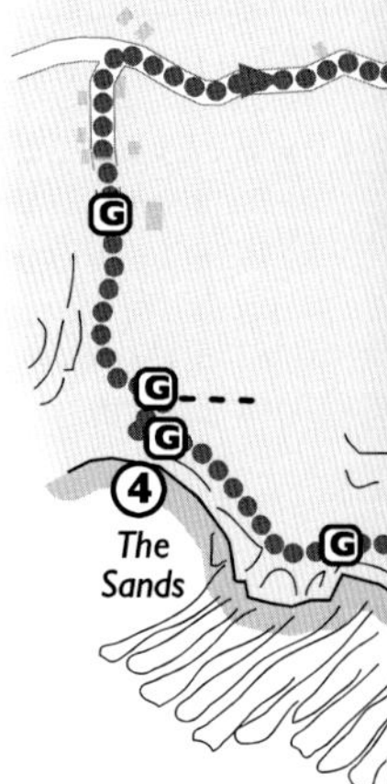

4 From here go through a kissing gate to follow the path leading inland and this forms part of a long standing diversion. Go through another kissing gate and turn LEFT. Follow the track ahead and then round to pass through a kissing gate where you bear RIGHT on a track, through a gate, then leading up a valley, known as the Slade. At the T junction, turn RIGHT to walk along a lane where there are superb views towards the sea. Follow this through to Oxwich Green. Continue ahead until you reach a junction.

5 Cross a stone stile on the right and head across the field towards Oxwich Castle. Cross a second stile and turn LEFT on the track. The entrance to the castle is on the right to the rear of the car park (there's a charge for entry). When you have visited return to the track and head down the lane. Turn RIGHT to walk down the road to the crossroads in the village. Continue ahead for the bus stop and car park.

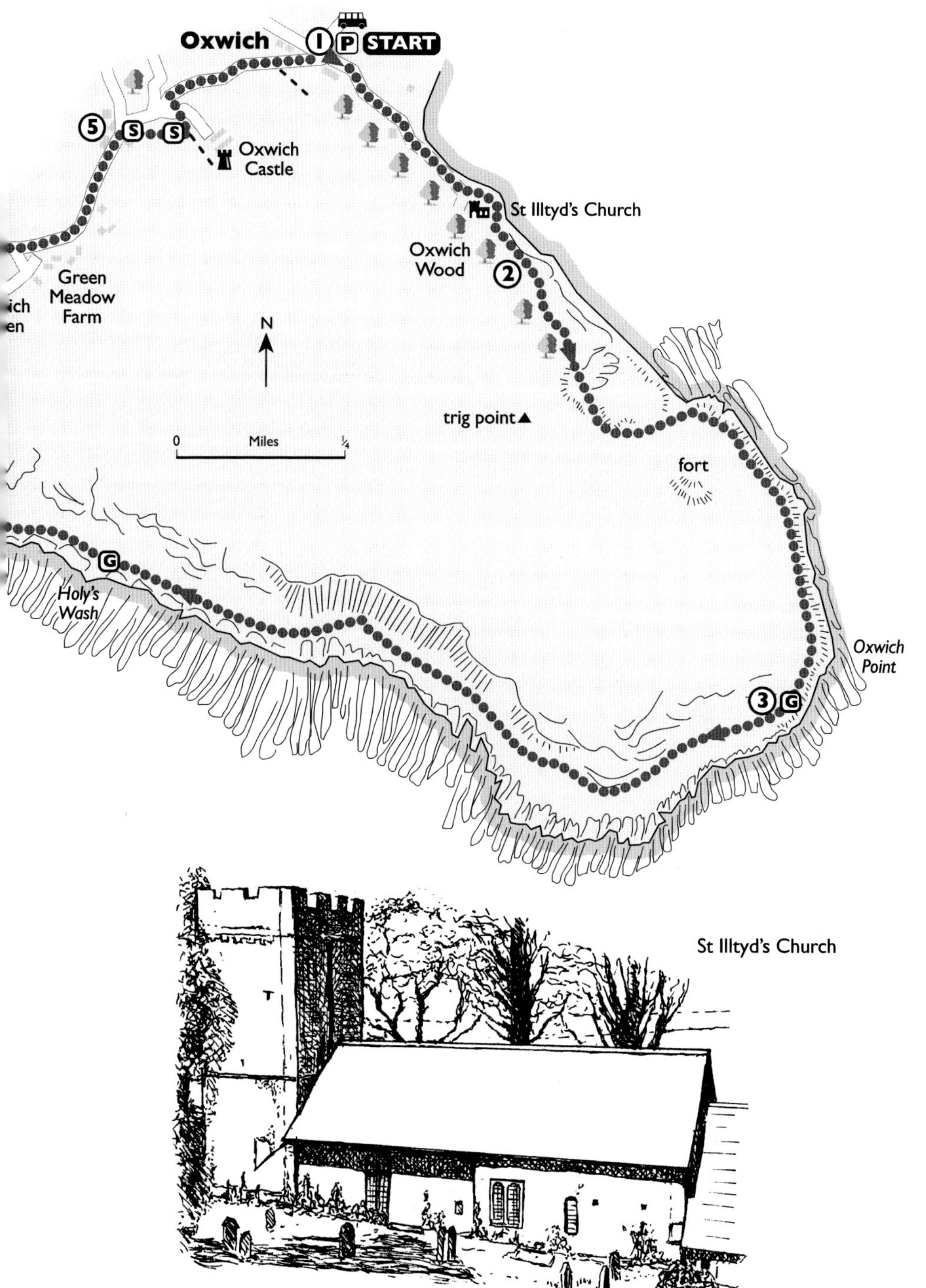

St Illtyd's Church

WALK 15

PORT-EYNON BAY

DESCRIPTION This is a moderate 3½ mile walk which passes behind the dunes at Port Eynon, popping by the RNLI shop and centre, and through Lower Horton. There's a climb up a wooded gully to Western Slade and then the path follows a track to Slade, returning along a fine section of the Wales Coast Path to Port Eynon Bay.

START Car park and bus stop nearby, Port Eynon, SS 467852.

DIRECTIONS There's a daily bus in summer and Mondays to Saturdays in winter (118/119 connecting to 115/117). The bus stop is next to the car park in Port Eynon near the roundabout.

1 Start at the roundabout where you turn RIGHT to walk by the shop and cafes. The path runs along boards through dunes to a track which bends left and right to then continue ahead. You will encounter cross paths but keep ahead, past a waterworks building, and into a car park at Horton and onward to the RNLI centre. Pass to the left of it heading across a green to join a lane.

2 Turn RIGHT to walk along it to its end. At this point, go LEFT, through a green bridle gate situated to the right of a garage. Climb up through the woodland to cross a stile and keep ahead.

3 Go through a kissing gate and turn RIGHT to follow the track to another kissing gate by a barred gate and through the farm buildings at Western Slade. Continue along the track passing through a gate to reach a lane at Eastern Slade.

4 Turn RIGHT at a junction to descend a lane, passing through a gap by a gate and onto a track. At a fork go RIGHT on the Wales Coast Path to soon pass through a gate. Follow the track downhill.

5 At the bottom, turn RIGHT and follow the well-worn Wales Coast path to reach a gate at Lower Horton leading onto the lane used on the way out. Continue to the green and cut LEFT, as waymarked to the beach and return to Port Eynon along the beach.

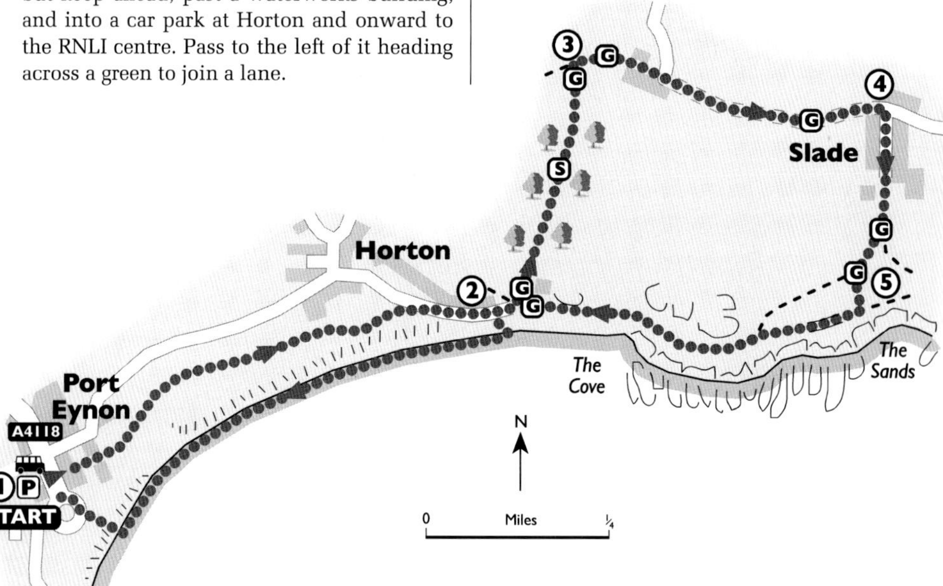

WALK 16

PORT EYNON HEADLAND

DESCRIPTION A moderate 3 mile circular. The walk rises up to Overton and along a grassy bridleway to join the Wales Coast Path returning on a dramatic section via Longhole, Overton Cliff and rising up to a monument dedicated to founder members of the Gower Society, on Port Eynon Headland. It passes near the remains of the Salt House (an old salt works) and a Youth Hostel on the return leg.

START Car park and bus stop nearby, Port Eynon, SS 467852.

DIRECTIONS There's a daily bus in summer and Mondays to Saturdays in winter (118/119 connecting to 115/117 at Scurlage). The bus stop is next to the car park in Port Eynon near the roundabout.

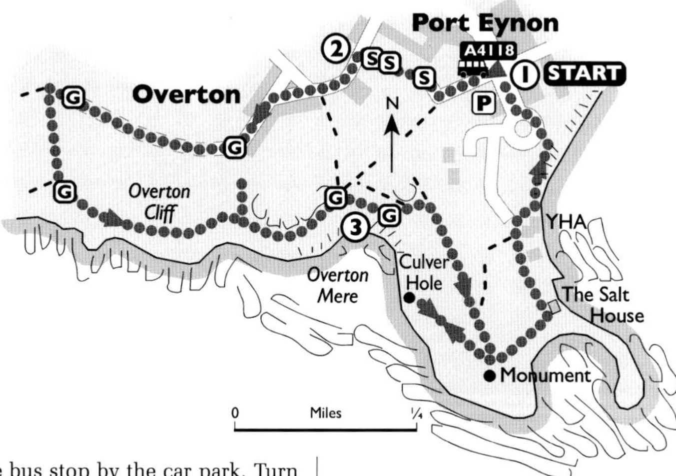

1 Start at the bus stop by the car park. Turn LEFT, then almost immediately LEFT towards the camping and caravan park and second LEFT to walk along a tarmac road between caravans. At the end of this you'll see a stile slightly right in line with a telegraph pole. Rise up to cross the stile and head just to the right of the pole to cross another stile. Keep ahead to climb a third stile and reach a lane. Go LEFT to pass New House farm.

2 At the junction at Overton green keep LEFT on a lane leading to a gap and gate onto a bridleway. Follow this to a bridle gate by a gate and a junction. Go LEFT on the Wales Coast Path to descend to Long Hole Cliff Nature Reserve. Turn LEFT through a kissing gate and pass beneath Overton Cliff on a narrow path; take care. It then skirts Overton Mere, bending RIGHT to a bridle gate; avoid left turns to Overton. The path now climbs steeply to the headland. Note that you can divert here to take a look a Culver Hole; however, keep away from the edge!

3 At the top follow the path ahead to the Gower Society monument, then peel off left to drop down stony path to a junction with a waymark post. You'll see the remains of the Salt House which at one time was a substantial producer of sea salt hereabouts. Go LEFT here then turn RIGHT at the next junction down to the Youth Hostel. From this point you walk back along the beach to the front and roundabout.

1 From the bus stop walk towards the sea, passing the car park, the Worm's Head Hotel and the National Trust Centre. Continue through a kissing gate and towards Worm's Head on a track. When this bends left walk slightly LEFT on a grassy path to join a drystone wall. Follow this ahead towards Fall Bay where the path curves LEFT to keep to high ground before dipping RIGHT into a gully; the path to the right leads to Mewslade Bay. Go through a kissing gate and rise up to a headland.

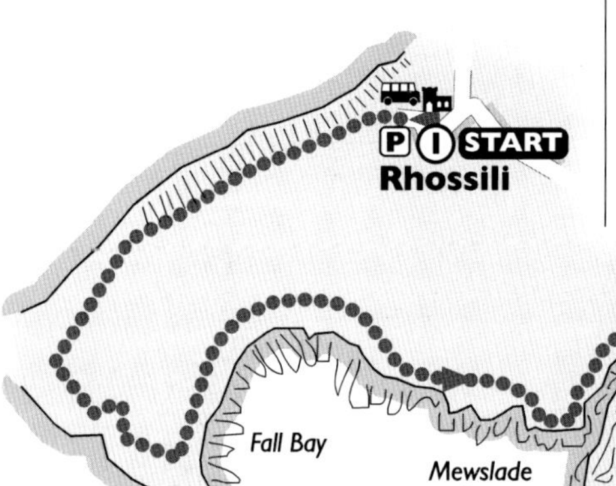

2 From here onwards follow a clear path passing a succession of headlands between drystone walls and fields to the left and cliffs to the right. You will also encounter gullies with bracken and bramble to wade through plus gorse banks. The path is clear on the ground with occasional gates where boundaries are crossed. There are paths off left to Pilton and Pilton Green which you ignore and some braids in places which soon come back to the main path. Follow the path for approximately 3 miles finally across Common Cliff to reach a junction with a waymark post.

3 Go RIGHT here to descend towards the coast again and a marker for Long Hole Cliff. Turn LEFT to follow a narrow path beneath Overton Cliff where neat footwork is required. The path runs along scree then, through a bridle gate then bends RIGHT around the edge of the nature reserve at Overton Mere, then through another bridle gate before making a climb up to the headland at Port Eynon.

4 Keep ahead along the headland to the Gower Society monument then head slightly LEFT down a rocky and stony path to a waymark post. Go LEFT here and then at the next junction turn RIGHT down to the Youth Hostel. Then walk along the beach into Port Eynon where the front leads up to a roundabout. The bus stop is a short distance up the road leading away from the beach.

5 If continuing to Scurlage, go right to pass by the shop and cafés along a boardwalk through the dunes. The path becomes a track and bends left and right and then ahead again. Continue ahead, crossing paths and by a water works into a car park at Horton. Keep to the right and walk ahead to the RNLI centre. Just before this turn LEFT to walk up to a lane and follow this up the hillside, ignoring a turn to the right, as far as a post box at a corner.

6 Go LEFT here and within 20 yards turn RIGHT as signposted to Scurlage. This track becomes a tarmac lane and comes to a junction. Cross over and follow the track ahead through a gate and then ahead to cross a stile by another gate. Go through a small pasture to cross a stile ahead and through

WALK 17

RHOSSILI, PORT EYNON & SCURLAGE

DESCRIPTION An energetic 9 mile linear walk along a spectacular section of the Wales Coast Path to Port Eynon and Horton with a short final section up a lane and through fields to Scurlage. There are superb views across headlands and cliffs with descents and climbs in and out of the gullies on this well waymarked route. Refreshments are available in Port Eynon and Scurlage.

START Bus stop at Rhossili, SS 416881.

FINISH Car park and adjacent bus stop, Port Eynon, SS 467852; or bus stop at Scurlage, SS 464876.

DIRECTIONS There's a daily bus (118/119) in summer and Mondays to Saturdays in winter from Swansea to Rhossili via Scurlage. There is a National Trust car park in Rhossili. Those wishing to finish their walk at Port Eynon can catch the connecting 115/117...but they are less frequent.

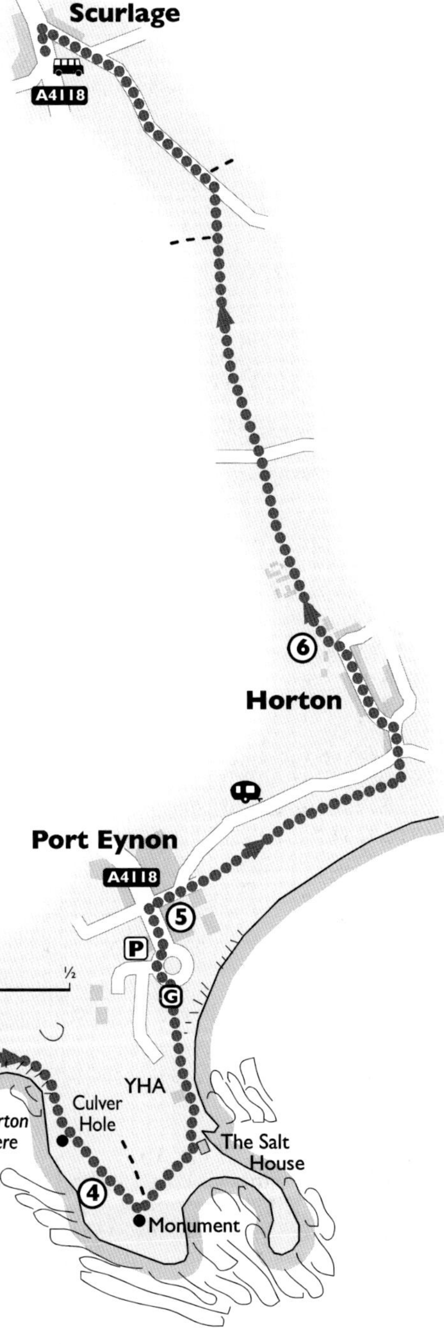

the next field to cross a stile by a gate, ahead again across another stile and then onward to a stile leading onto a track. Go LEFT to walk into Scurlage. Turn LEFT at the main road, the stop for Swansea is on the right and the stop for Rhossili is along the B4247 just before the fish and chip shop.

WALK 18

RHOSSILI, MEWSLADE BAY & WORM'S HEAD

DESCRIPTION This moderate 4½ mile walk goes from Rhossili through to Middleton between fields featuring medieval strip farming. It then descends towards Mewslade Bay where it picks up the Wales Coast Path back towards Worm's Head and Rhossili. There are great views at this point. For the most part this is easy walking but with a few climbs along the coast the walk is rated moderate. There are plenty of places for refreshment in Rhossili.

START Bus stop, Rhossili, SS 416881.

DIRECTIONS There's a daily bus (118/119) all year with Sunday/Bank Holiday buses in summer. There's only one bus stop in the village where the bus turns around. There is a National Trust car park in the village.

1 Start with the bus stop and shelter behind you. Go LEFT on the road and take the second turn on the RIGHT by a waymark sign on a telegraph pole and a litter bin. In a few yards reach a junction of tracks. Take the RIGHT fork and follow the enclosed track until you reach a Tir Gofal waymark sign on a stile to the LEFT.

2 Cross the stile and follow the left hand side of the field to a stile onto a track. Turn LEFT and follow the footpath route, mostly between hedges and crossing another two stiles. After the second stile take the RIGHT hand fork in the path. Cross a further six stiles on the route which is waymarked. On reaching a junction turn LEFT and follow the track to a junction with the B road at Middleton.

3 Turn RIGHT to walk on the pavement through the village. At the end of the pavement continue along the right hand side of the road for a few yards. Turn RIGHT on a path signed for Mewslade. Follow the enclosed path; look out for the notice on a gate about the wildlife. Continue along a track and go through a gate onto National Trust land.

4 Bear RIGHT on the Wales Coast Path and follow this for about 2 miles to the junction at the end of the drystone wall; the lookout station and Worm's Head is across to the left. Head slightly right on a grassy path to join a track which leads back to Rhossili with fine views across the bay.

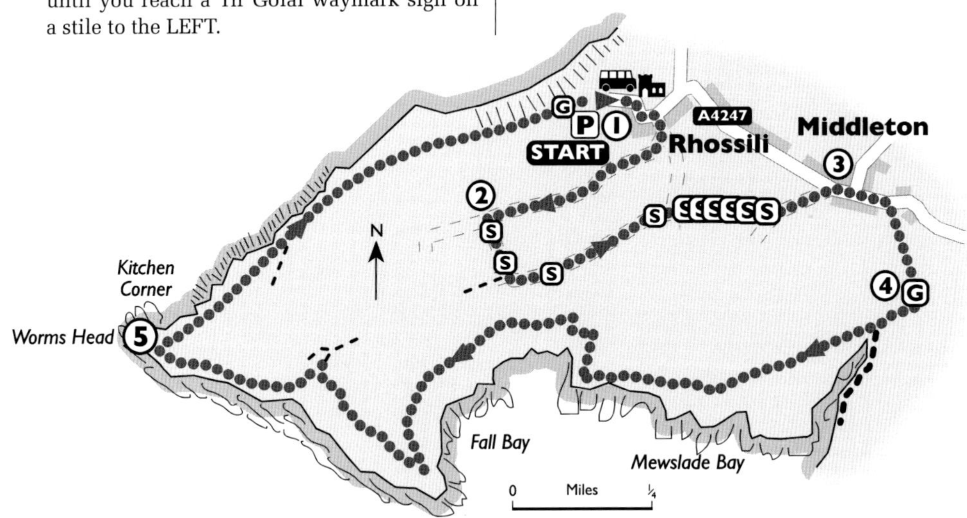

WALK 19

RHOSSILI DOWN & BEACH

DESCRIPTION This moderate 4½ mile circular walk passes by Rhossili church to climb the Down where there are superb viewpoints throughout. It descends to Hillend Burrows and there's an option to return at the foot of the down on a bridleway or to wander along one of the finest beaches in Wales. A simply sumptuous walk.

START Bus stop, Rhossili, SS 416881.

DIRECTIONS There's a daily bus (118/119) in summer and Mondays to Saturdays in winter. There's a National Trust car park in the village.

1 Turn LEFT from the bus shelter to head inland along a path to the left of a garage and then to the left of the church. Turn LEFT on meeting a track, passing a standing stone to the right. Ignore the waymarked gate on the left but continue ahead to a second waymarked gate leading onto the Down. Head up the hillside; there's a small building to the left. Go up steps and climb up to the top. The path bends slightly left to the Beacon trig point.

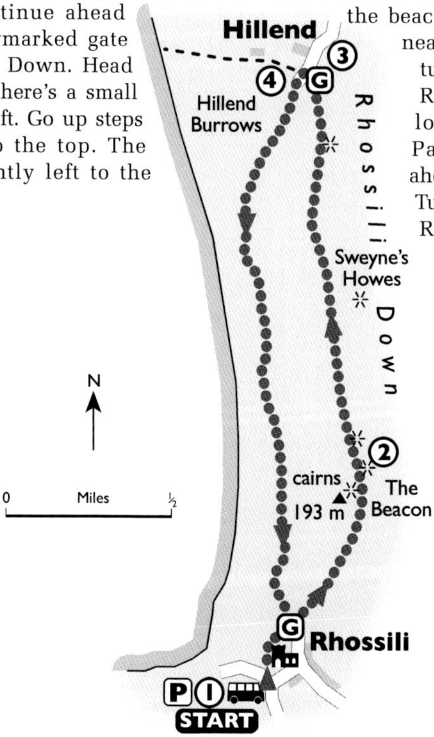

2 Continue along the ridge for well over a mile. The path forks and there's a waymark. Keep LEFT here to pass by the remains of a wartime radar station before climbing again. Now descend, sharply in places and slightly LEFT down the hillside to Hillend Burrows.

3 If you prefer to follow the bridleway at the foot of the Downs then DO NOT go through the gate at the base onto the lane. Instead turn sharp LEFT to follow the bridleway, wet in places but with great views over the beach, back to Rhossili. The path is clear enough and there's one last climb as you make your way back to a point near Rhossili church where you retrace your steps.

4 Alternatively, go through the gate onto the lane at Hillend Burrows. Cross over the lane and turn LEFT to follow the route through the camping area, and past a shop and café (on the left) to a car parking plot. Continue on a path through the dunes to the beach. Turn LEFT and wander along the beach back towards Rhossili. On nearing the cliffs at the far end turn LEFT to go up steps. Bear RIGHT through a gate and follow the path to another gate. Pass through it and proceed ahead to a junction with a road. Turn LEFT for the bus stop and RIGHT for the car park.

WALK 20

LLANDDEWI & RHOSSILI

DESCRIPTION An easy 4 mile linear walk with only one climb skirting the edge of Rhossili Down following an old drover's trail. Do not attempt after very wet weather as there's a ford to cross. Llanddewi is an ancient settlement and historians also note that there was a castle here in medieval times as well as the church; the latter is open to visitors in the summer months. The path follows the Gower Way for the most part, passing farms that no longer prosper in a part of the Gower that has not given over to tourism. The old way runs between pastures with mixed farming. It climbs the southern flank of Rhossili Down to enter the village through fields. There are refreshments and the National Trust Centre and shop at Rhossili.

START Bus stop, Llanddewi Turn, SS 463889.

FINISH Bus Stop, Rhossili, SS 416881.

DIRECTIONS There's a daily bus (118/119) in summer and Mondays to Saturdays in winter connecting Swansea to Llanddewi Turn and Rhossili.

1 Start at the bus stop just beyond Llanddewi Turn; there's a shelter on one side and simply a verge on the other. Cross to the shelter and walk along the verge to Llanddewi corner and road junction. Just beyond go LEFT over a bridge and stile. Head slightly RIGHT over the next field to cross a stone stile onto a lane. Go ahead to walk between an old farm on the left and St David's church on the right – *it dates from the 14thC but with much restoration in Victorian times.*

2 Pass through a gate and follow the concrete track until it eventually bends left. You, however, continue ahead on a green way, known as Kingshall Lane, through a barred gate and on another track. Keep ahead to pass by the 16thC Old Henllys, then through two gates onto a wide green way. This gives out at a stile by a gate into a field. Head half LEFT across to exit at a bridle gate. Proceed ahead through another bridle gate. Keep ahead with a hedge on the right. Follow the track leading off slightly right and through a barred gate. Continue ahead and through a bridle gate.

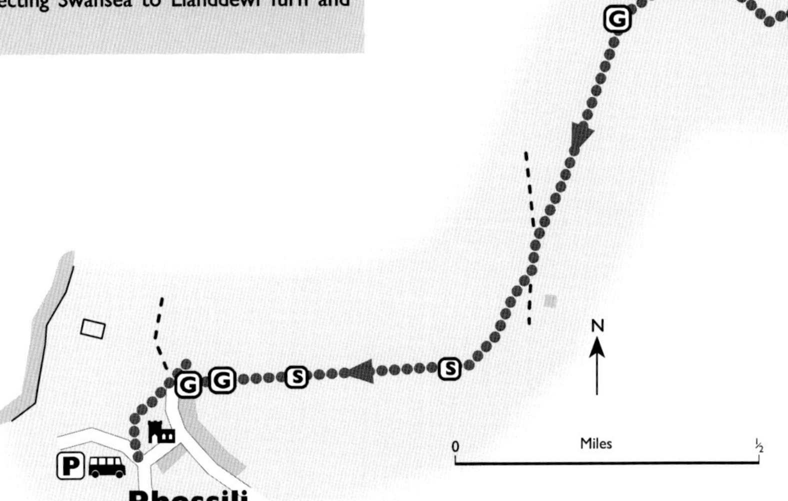

3 Follow the track by the bucolic ruins of Kingshall farm, through a gate and over a ford. Proceed ahead and the track soon bends left through a barred gate onto the down. Keep ahead now to climb gently up to a bungalow and Fernhill farm. Just beyond turn RIGHT, at a waymark post, to climb up the bank to a second waymark post. Keep LEFT here to rise through bracken and gorse. At the next junction keep LEFT for about 50 yards on a track and then pass to the right of an enclosed reservoir tank. Keep ahead to cross a stile and then it opens up. Keep LEFT and then RIGHT to walk through wet ground to cross a stile into a field.

4 Head very slightly RIGHT across a field to climb a stile and you'll see the rooftops of Rhossili dwellings ahead. Cross a stile and head down the field to a bridle gate by a barred gate. Go ahead through the gate and walk along a track to a road. Turn RIGHT down a track and then cut LEFT and then RIGHT to walk to the bus stop in Rhossili.

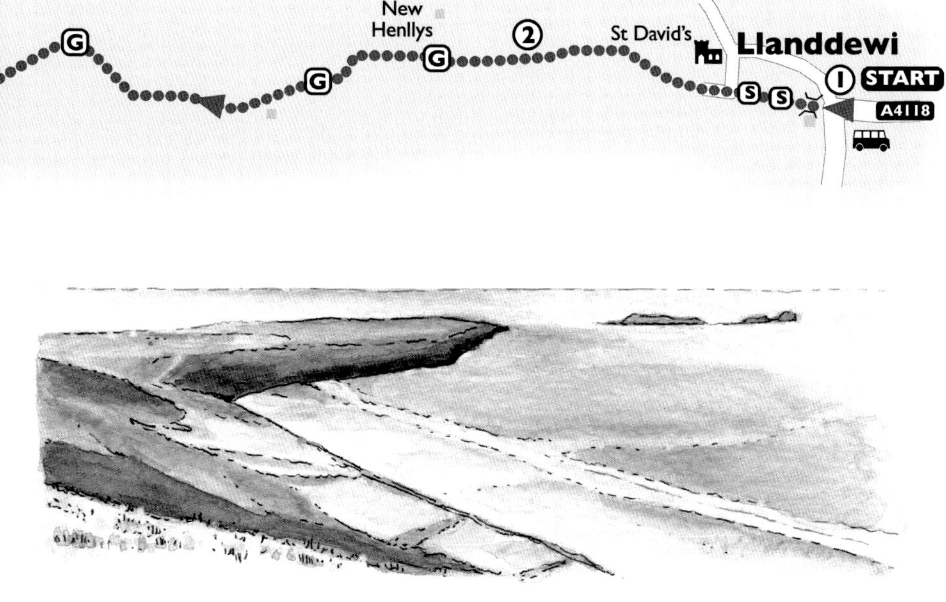

Rhossili Bay

WALK 21

LLANGENNITH, RHOSSILI BAY & BURRY HOLMS

DESCRIPTION A varied moderate walk of 6 miles, starting from the pretty village of Llangennith (with ancient church and also a pub). The walk then goes through attractive countryside below Rhossili Down to reach the northern part of breathtaking Rhossili bay, including a visit to Burry Holms, a romantic little tidal island and site of an iron age hill fort. The route then joins an attractive cliff-top stretch of the Wales Coast Path giving views ahead to Broughton Bay and beyond, before turning inland to cross quiet pastures of Llangennith Moors back to the start. Note that Burry Holms is only accessible for 2 or 3 hours either side of low tide (so check the times of tides before starting) – at other times the walk will still be varied and enjoyable. The walk can be linked to Walk 22 (see Section 5 below) to make a longer 8½ mile walk.

START Bus stop at the King's Head, Llangennith, SS 429915.

DIRECTIONS 115 and 116 buses (Mon – Sat) and the 116 Gower Explorer (Summer Sundays) call at Llangennith. If coming by car, park at Hillend camp site, about a mile south-west of Llangennith, and start the walk at Section 3, completing 1 and 2 at the end..

1 From the church (*dating from the 12thC and worth a visit*), walk down the road next to it with the church on your left. At the end of the road, continue ahead over a bridge on a track, soon forking left across grass to follow another track/path. This leads through a gate to pass a National Trust sign and soon reaches a cross roads of bridleways. Turn RIGHT.

2 Follow this path near to the edge of the down, ignoring paths to left and right, until you reach a gate on the RIGHT leading to Hillend camp site. Turn through this, cross over the lane and turn LEFT down through the campsite to the parking place for non-campers.

3 Join the footpath situated towards the right hand side of the car park and follow the walkway between fences to the beach. Turn RIGHT and follow the beach towards the rocky line of Spaniard Rocks about a

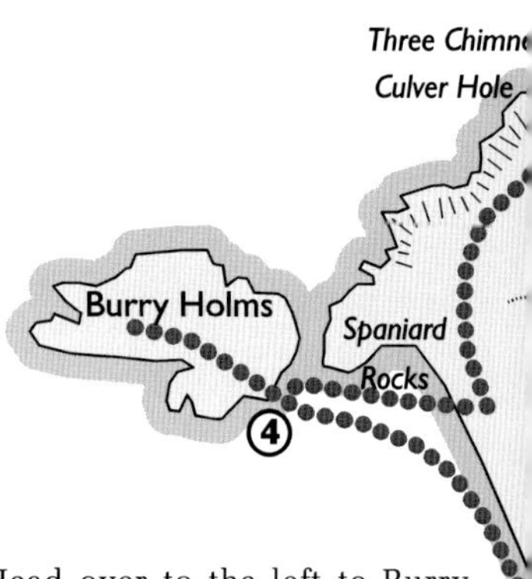

mile away. Head over to the left to Burry Holms and look for a sandy rock-free route to the island – but MAKE SURE there is time for a visit – see DESCRIPTION above. *When exploring the island you will find the remains of a hill fort and ditch, the ruins of an old chapel and lots of places for a picnic or just for sitting and looking out.*

4 Return to the beach and go to the far end of the rocks on your left. Turn LEFT up the Coast Path and follow the waymarked route along the cliffs and through the dunes. After a while you will spot a secluded sandy beach below you to the left. This is Blue Pool Bay, so named as it has a very deep rockpool which adventurous people jump into. As you get near the end of the bay, just before a waymark post, there is a narrow path going down on your LEFT to the bay; if you walk a little way down it, you'll see the pool down on your left. The rest of the route down is extremely steep – and involves scrambling over rocks near the bottom, so is only suitable for the very sure-footed and nimble walker.

5 Soon the Coast Path passes a footpath leading to the left going to a promontory called Twlc Point; this makes an optional diversion, and you can return on another path joining the route a little further on. Bear RIGHT into the caravan site, and again at a three-way post, leaving the Coast Path and going through the site. (If you want to join Walk 22 here, then turn LEFT at the three-way post; walk down and out of the caravan site to cross a grassy patch leading to the beach. Turn RIGHT to walk along the beach and join section 3 of walk 22.) Immediately after passing a small car park on the right go through a kissing gate on the RIGHT, next to a large gate. Follow the good track ahead, and when you reach a fence, do not turn sharply left over a stile but soon turn LEFT over another stile. Continue ahead over three stiles, then through a kissing gate. Now keep close to the fence/hedge on your left over a succession of stiles and kissing gates until finally you reach a gate leading to a road. Bear LEFT up to a mini-roundabout and turn RIGHT. There is a bus stop immediately on your right, or you can walk along the road for a minute or two back to the start.

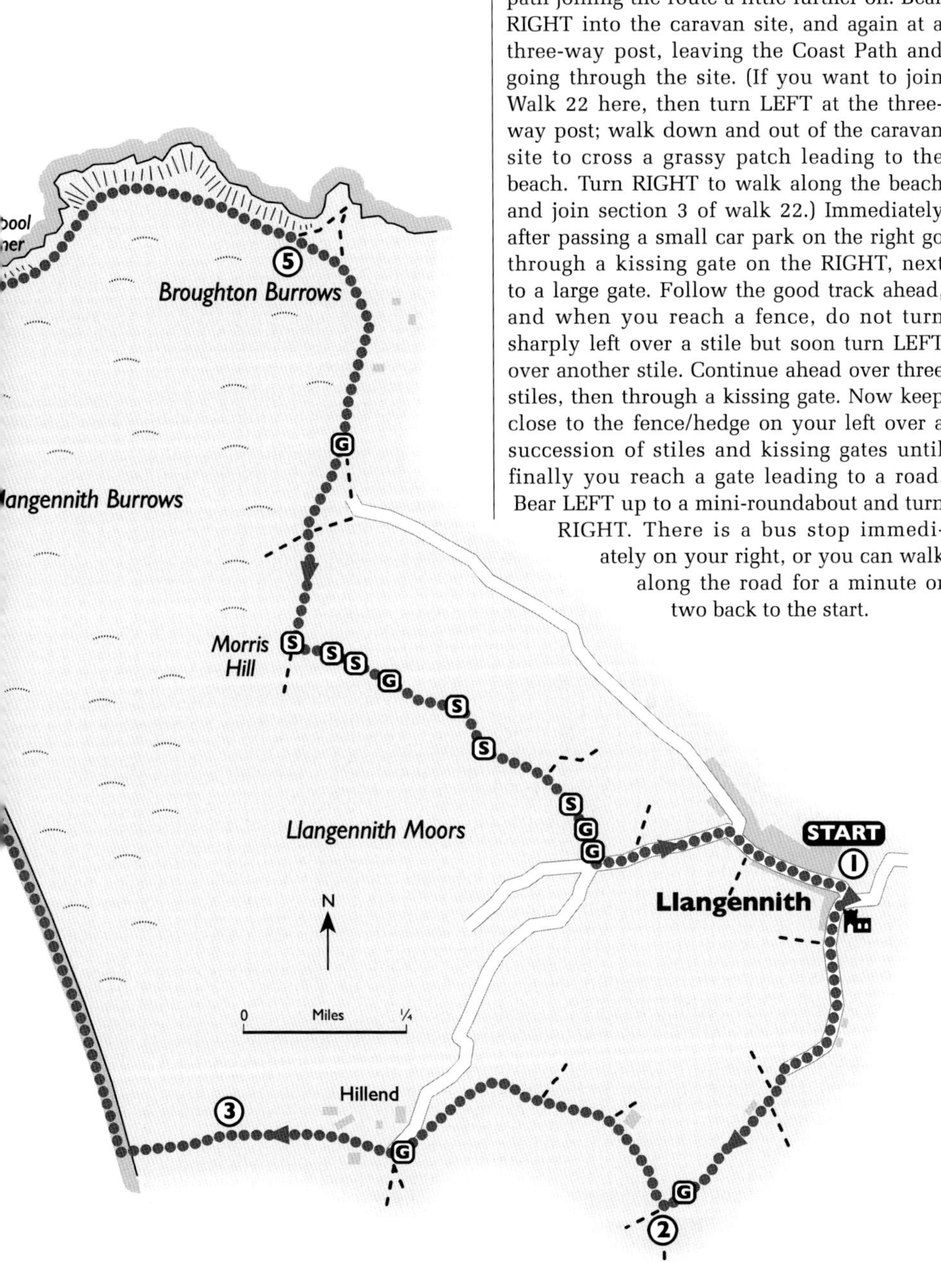

WALK 22

BROUGHTON BAY

DESCRIPTION An easy walk of about 3½ miles that can best be enjoyed at low tide. A quiet lane leads from Llanmadoc Village to enclosed sand dunes and then to the wide sandy beach of Broughton Bay – less famous than Rhossili Bay but also very impressive. The route passes two Tors (rocky promontories) and then approaches a third one which has over the years become separated from the sea by moving sands. A gentle ascent next to attractive woodland brings you back to Llanmadoc. Refreshments are available in Llanmadoc (see section 4 below). You can easily extend this walk to include Whiteford Sands by not turning right off the beach in Section 3 below and instead picking up the last 3 miles of Walk 23.

START Bus stop at Llanmadoc Green, SS 441933.

DIRECTIONS 115 and 116 buses (Mon – Sat) and the 116 Gower Explorer (Summer Sundays) call at Llanmadoc Green. There is a car park at Cwm Ivy, SS 440935; from here walk back towards the village to reach the bus stop..

1 From the bus stop walk westwards, away from the village, passing another green to reach the junction by the church; turn LEFT, signposted towards Broughton Beach. (From the car park, follow the lane back uphill to the junction by the church and turn RIGHT.) Follow the lane for about ½ mile and turn RIGHT over a cattle grid by the entrance to Whiteford Bay Leisure Park, with a footpath sign to Broughton Beach. At the end of the mobile home site, turn LEFT through a gate(signed to the beach).

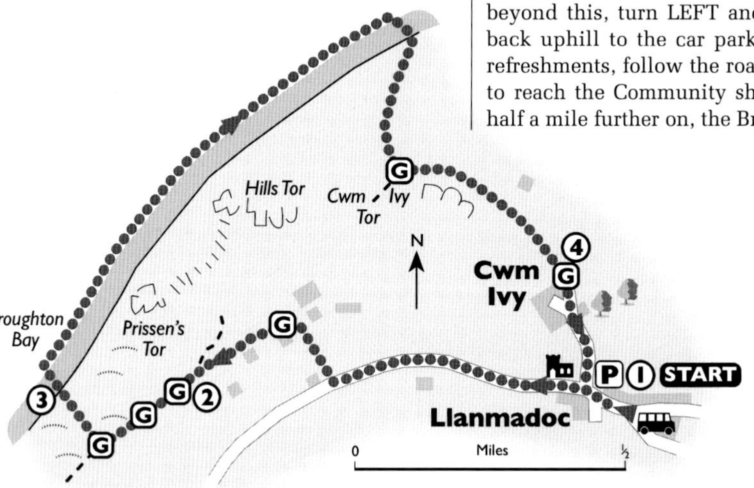

2 Soon join the Wales Coast Path coming in from the right. Follow the Coast Path round to the left, then to the right. Go through a gate and past another entrance to the Leisure Park and past a sewage pumping station. (Soon pass a track on the left leading in a minute or two to a café – seasonal opening only.) Keep ahead through a gate and round to the right through another (leaving the Coast Path) to the beach. Turn RIGHT.

3 Pass a rocky promontory (Prissen's Tor), then another (Hill's Tor). In about 10 minutes you will see another Tor (Cwm Ivy Tor) set back above the sand dunes on your right. *(If you want to extend the walk, don't turn right as below but instead stay on the beach; you are now at the beginning of Section 3 of walk 23.)* Before long turn sharply RIGHT along a clear track (rejoining the Coast Path) with Cwm Ivy Tor now ahead slightly to your left. Follow the path round to the left to reach, and go through, a gate. Turn LEFT.

4 Follow the track uphill, passing through a gate out of National Trust land. Just beyond this, turn LEFT and follow the lane back uphill to the car park and village. For refreshments, follow the road past two greens to reach the Community shop and café and, half a mile further on, the Britannia Inn.

WALK 23

WHITEFORD NATIONAL NATURE RESERVE

DESCRIPTION This is an easy 5 mile walk, starting from Llanmadoc village.It follows a quiet route down from the village past Cwm Ivy Tor (see walk 22) to reach the huge peaceful expanse of Whiteford Sands, adjoining Whiteford Burrows, which are renowned for wildlife, especially birds and flowers. The walk also goes close to a remarkable old lighthouse, the last remaining cast-iron sea-washed lighthouse in Europe, not everyone's idea of beauty but nevertheless Grade II listed and a scheduled ancient monument. The walk returns through woodland, with many conifers but also quite varied. Llanmadoc has a village café and a pub.

START Bus stop at Llanmadoc Green, SS 441933.

DIRECTIONS 115 and 116 buses (Mon – Sat) and the 116 Gower Explorer (Summer Sundays) call at Llanmadoc Green. There is a car park at Cwm Ivy, SS 440935; the walk passes this, so on leaving the car park turn RIGHT and ignore the first two sentences of Section 1 below.

1 From the bus stop walk westwards,away from the village, passing another green on the left. At the junction by the church take the right fork and descend the lane, passing the car park on the right. On reaching a group of houses, follow the lane round to the left, looking for a National Trust sign on a gate on the right.

2 Turn RIGHT through the gate and go down the lane and along the track, passing a junction with a right turn. The rocky cliff of Cwm Ivy Tor is on your left. At the next junction, turn RIGHT through a gate. Follow the sandy path/track as it bends round to the right.

3 Walk along the beach ahead.The iron lighthouse can be seen in the distance on the left. After about 1½ miles the route goes round Whiteford Point, with dunes on your right. At the end of the dunes, bear half RIGHT towards the first group of conifers. Look for noticeboards just to the left of the conifers – one of these is a National Nature Reserve sign. About 40 yards before this sign, turn RIGHT along a track into the trees.

4 Follow the main track as it winds its way through a variety of conifers, dunes and open land. After going through three well separated gates, the path eventually passes a National Trust bunkhouse on the right, and then Burrows Cottage (also a National Trust holiday cottage). Go through a final gate and turn LEFT, retracing your steps back to Llanmadoc. Refreshments are available at the village shop/café, a little way past the bus stop, or at the Britannia Inn, about ½ mile further on.

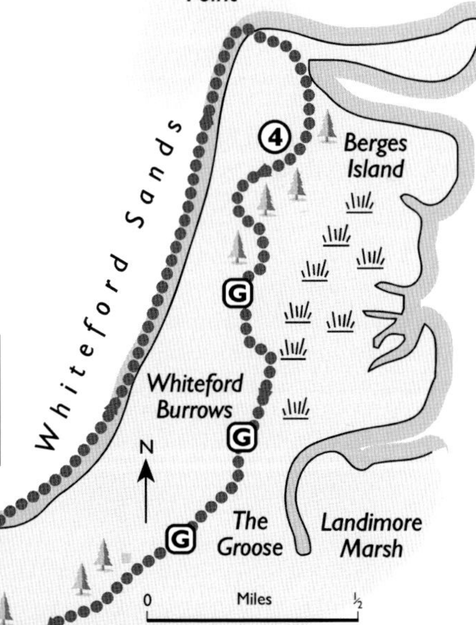

WALK 24

LLANMADOC VILLAGE, WOODS, MARSHLAND & SEA WALL

DESCRIPTION A moderate 3½ mile walk, starting from Llanmadoc village. Descending the main street past the village shop and café, the route then passes through attractive woodland`. After a short section of lane and track, the route passes between forestry and marshland. A right turn leads to a path along a medieval sea wall between salt and freshwater marshes, with good views of both; however salt water is now encroaching on the freshwater side (see Note below), leading to significant changes in the ecosystem.

START Bus stop at Llanmadoc Green, SS 441933.

DIRECTIONS 115 and 116 buses (Mon – Sat) and the 116 Gower Explorer (Summer Sundays) call at Llanmadoc Green. There is a car park at Cwm Ivy, SS 440935; from here walk back towards the village to reach the bus stop.

NOTE At the time of writing (Spring 2016) there is a breach in the wall on Section 5 of the walk as indicated on the map. This part of the route is therefore impassable. It is possible that a bridge will be installed across the gap but until this happens you can walk as far as the breach from either side but will then have to retrace your steps. The wall is still worth walking on, and the gap gives an impressive insight into the power of the sea.

1 Walk along on the main village street, soon passing the village shop and café (highly recommended). Ignore the first footpath sign on the left and continue downhill.Soon after passing a house called 'Dane's Dyke' on the right, turn LEFT on the side lane and follow this for a short distance to a gate on the right.

2 Go through the gate and follow the track downhill through woodland. Pass through a further gate and follow the track ahead to the right of a shed and then to the right of a house. Go through another gate and continue ahead, ignoring a right turn. Pass to the right of a cottage. Shortly after this, the track becomes a path that continues through woodland.

3 Pass a set of steps on the left, and a few yards further on turn LEFT through a kissing gate and follow the path along the lower edge of the wood, passing through a second kissing gate into the nature reserve. Go through a third gate at the end of the wood and follow the track past an old building on the right. Head half LEFT up a drive to a lane.

4 Turn RIGHT on the lane and follow this past houses. When the lane bends round to the left, look for a gate with a National Trust sign set back on the RIGHT. Go through this and down the lane, which in due course becomes a track, to reach a waymarked junction. Turn RIGHT through the gate and follow the track between forestry on the left and marshes on the right. Pass through a gate.

5 About 100 yards after the gate turn RIGHT through a kissing gate to follow the Wales Coast Path along the top of a medieval sea wall separating Cwm Ivy freshwater marsh on the right from the salt marsh on the left. See note above before section 1. If there is now a bridge, cross it and at the end of the wall follow the path round to the right to go through a kissing gate. Ignore the gate on the right (which you went through earlier) and continue ahead for a short way.

6 ***This section is only recommended in dry weather as the final track leading to the road can get very muddy. If in doubt, ignore the flight of steps on the right and continue ahead, retracing your route in sections 1 and 2 above.*** At a waymark sign turn RIGHT through a gate and go up a flight of steps. Follow the path through the wood, ascending steps on the steeper sections, to a stile into a field. Head across the field to a kissing gate in the diagonally opposite corner. Continue along the left hand side of the next narrow field to a kissing gate leading on to an

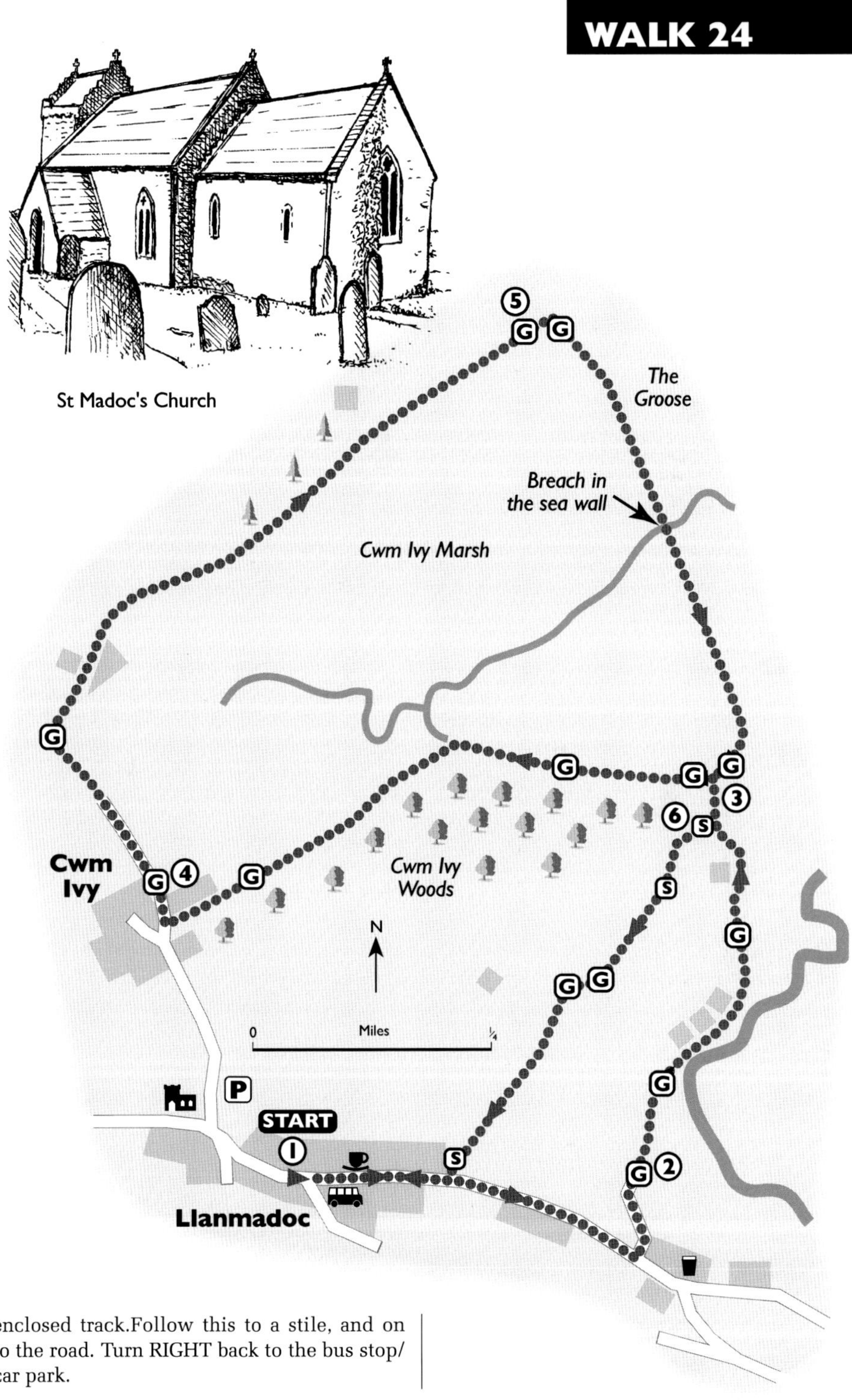

enclosed track.Follow this to a stile, and on to the road. Turn RIGHT back to the bus stop/ car park.

WALK 25
LLANMADOC HILL

DESCRIPTION A moderate 3½ mile walk from Llanmadoc Village up to Llanmadoc Hill. Passing through the site of a prehistoric hill fort, the route follows the ridge along to the top of the hill, with spectacular views all round – over the tidal estuary to Carmarthenshire, the beaches and rocky tors of the coast line, Rhossili Down and Worm's Head, and the farmlands of central Gower. Refreshments are available in Llanmadoc (see Section 1 below).
START Bus stop at Llanmadoc Green, SS 441933.
DIRECTIONS 115 and 116 buses (Mon – Sat) and the 116 Gower Explorer (Summer Sundays) call at Llanmadoc Green. There is a car park at Cwm Ivy, SS 440935; from here walk back towards the village to reach the bus stop.

1 The excellent community shop and café is a short way ahead on the road back into the village (and the Britannia Inn about half a mile further on) but for the walk take the no-through road from the back of the green (to the right of the road to the shop) past several houses, then round to the right where the lane soon becomes a track.

2 Follow the track uphill to the open access hillside. Immediately after passing the gate to a house on the left (Hill House), take the first turning on the LEFT up a grassy path through bracken.Follow this path, ignoring turnings, to reach the junction with a stony track.

3 Walk ahead up the stony track until you reach the banks and ditches of the hillfort.Soon after the path starts to bend left towards a gate, bear RIGHT between two rocks on a grassy path into the hillfort. Continue up through the fort to the ridge; the track meanders towards a trig point, which you will see ahead on the skyline. Maintain direction until you reach this.

4 Having admired the views from the trig point (the hill ahead and slightly to your left is Rhossili Down), continue in the same direction past a cairn and bear RIGHT past a toposcope (worth pausing here too). Continue down the path, ignoring a right fork, until you reach a junction with a lot of large rocks ahead. Here turn RIGHT on a grassy path that leads back along the hillside, with views of the estuary and Carmarthenshire coast beyond.

5 Eventually, come in sight of three houses on the left at the edge of the open access land. Turn LEFT down a narrow path towards the second house and turn RIGHT on a track. At a junction of tracks, keep ahead along the track you came up on, soon getting back to the village.

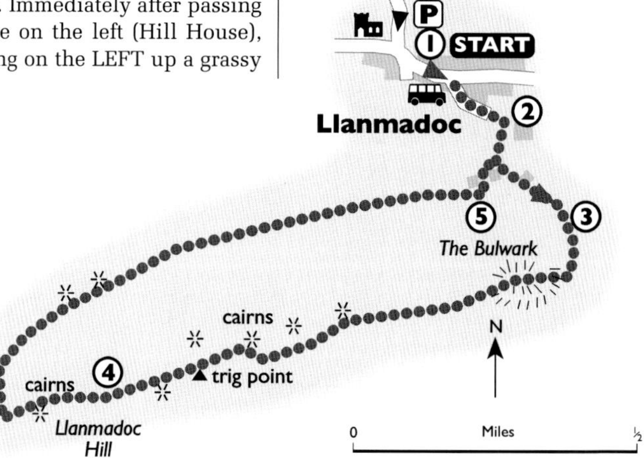

WALK 26

GELLI-HIR WOOD

DESCRIPTION Gelli-Hir wood is one of the reserves owned by the Wildlife Trust of South and West Wales. It is a partly ancient wood, dating from before the 1600s, and contains an attractive abundance of broad leaved trees and plenty of fallen and rotting timber to support fungi, etc. Butterflies and damsel flies can be seen in summer. There is a secluded pond with a bird hide nearby. The walk described below is about a mile. (For a longer walk which includes this wood, see Walk 30.)

START Roadside lay-by at SS 562924.

DIRECTIONS Going west on the B4271 from the junction with the A4118, turn right after about 1½ miles, signed to Cilonen. In about ½ mile, soon after the cattle grid, there is a small lay-by on the left, and the entrance to the reserve is on the right. There is a stop (but no sign) at Cilonen Turn for the 119 bus between Swansea and Rhossili. Bus users may prefer to make this a linear walk by completing the last part (Sections 7 – 12) of walk 30 to finish in Three Crosses (or to do the whole of walk 30).

1 Follow the track through a gate into the reserve and after a short distance turn RIGHT along a grassy track through the wood and then round to the left. Continue along the main path, crossing two small footbridges. Ignore a left turn. Cross over a junction of paths and continue ahead to reach the junction with a wider track.

2 Turn RIGHT and follow the wider track, bearing left on this when it nears the edge of the wood. Keep to the main track and cross two more small footbridges. At a junction with a wide track turn RIGHT. At the next junction turn LEFT to reach the bird hide on the right and pond on the left. (To get into the hide, return down the path you came on for a short way, and take the first turning sharply LEFT. To get a better view of the pond, turn LEFT as you approach it, so that it's on your right. In a few steps you reach the sluice gate.)

3 To return to the entrance, start back along the outward route past the turning to the hide. Bear RIGHT at the first junction and then continue ahead on the main track back to where you started.

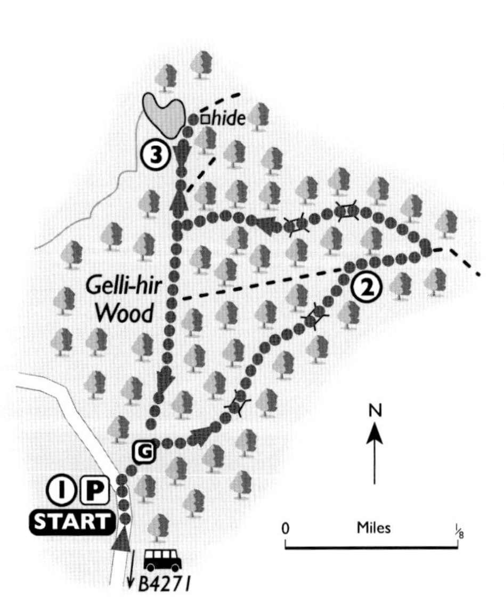

The pond at Gelli-hir

WALK 27

BURRY PILL & TOR GRO

DESCRIPTION This is a moderate 6 mile walk (but with one steep climb, which could be omitted) which passes through a wide range of contrasting scenery, starting with extensive views from Llanmadoc Hill, then descending through woodland to pass a 14thC church. It then follows an ancient wooded valley, reaching a notable old packhorse bridge. From here there is an ascent to the top of an area of common land (owned by the National Trust) with even more spectacular views. The walk continues to the peaceful hamlet of Landimore, and then takes a route with an interesting contrast of scenery – woodland on the left and salt marsh grazing on the right. Finally you return through woodland and pasture to reach a quiet road leading back to Llanmadoc, via a pub and the village café.

START Bus stop at Llanmadoc Green, SS 441933.

DIRECTIONS 115 and 116 buses (Mon – Sat) and 116 Gower Explorer (Summer Sundays) call at Llanmadoc Green. There is a car park at Cwm Ivy, SS 440935; from here walk back towards the village to reach the bus stop.

1 The excellent community shop and café is a short way ahead on the road back into the village (and the Britannia Inn about half a mile further on) but for the walk take the no-through road from the back of the green (to the right of the road to the shop) past several houses, then round to the right where the lane soon becomes a track.

2 Follow the track uphill to the open access hillside. Immediately after passing the gate to a house on the left (Hill House), take the first turning on the LEFT up a grassy path through bracken. Follow this path, ignoring turnings, to reach the junction with a stony track.

3 Turn LEFT and follow the track downhill. Opposite a house called Stormy Castle on the right, fork LEFT down a grassy track aiming for a white house at the bottom. Cross the road and take the waymarked route between trees, just to the left of the house. Follow the old track down through the woods, keeping close to the fence on your left. On reaching a drive, follow this down to the road. Turn RIGHT and follow the road, soon reaching St Cadoc's church on the left. *The church is known as the 'Cathedral of Gower' and has a notable 14thC entrance doorway.* Continue a short way further along the road and turn RIGHT along a waymarked footpath towards Stembridge.

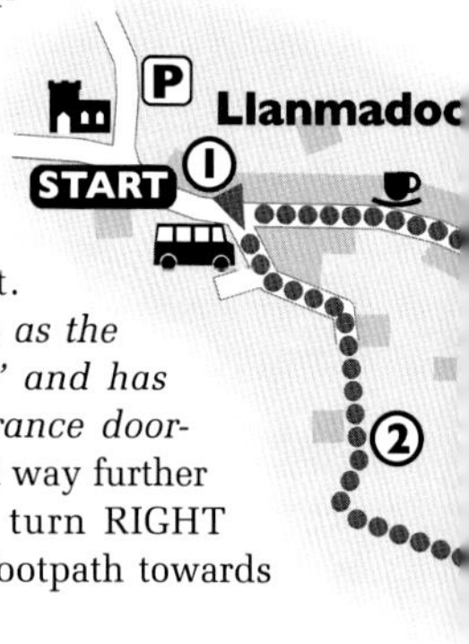

4 Follow the drive towards Bridge pottery for a few yards, then go through the gate on the left. Head along the right hand edge of the field to a stile. Cross this and follow the path ahead through the wood, crossing a second stile. At a two-way waymark post, take the right fork, soon leaving the woods. Now keep along the right hand side of the fields, going through a total of three gates. The third one takes you onto a bridleway going to left and right, and an information board. *On your right is the 17thC packhorse bridge, a hint that this region used to be a hive of activity, with several mills along the Burry Pill. The word pill probably comes from the Welsh word pwl, meaning an inlet or pool, but here pill means a river.*

5 Turn RIGHT over the old bridge and follow the bridleway round to the left; then look for a path going steeply uphill to the top of Ryers Down, where there is a trig point; there are extensive views all round. Descend by the same route, cross the packhorse bridge and turn RIGHT through a gate. The route now goes along the right hand edge of five fields keeping close to the Pill on your right, crossing a number of stiles and, eventually, going through a gate into a field with a house ahead. Here head for a gate just to the left of the house, go through this onto the drive

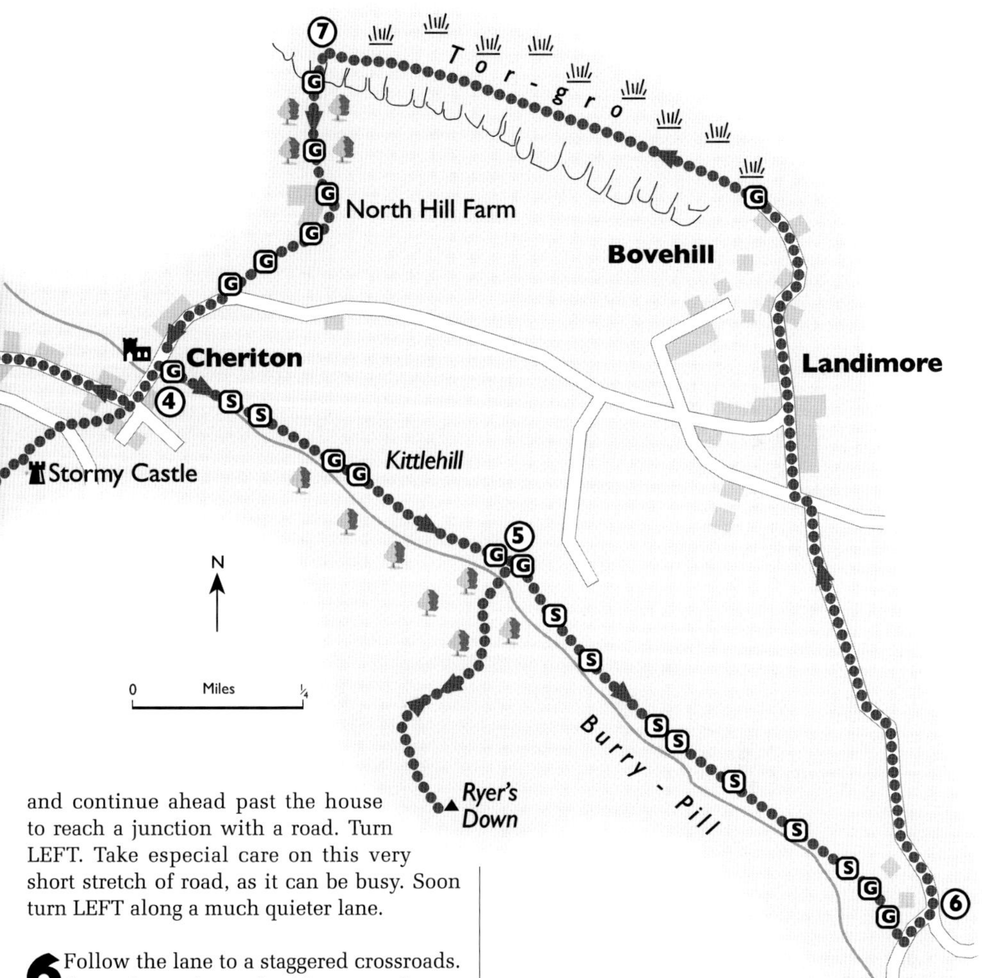

and continue ahead past the house to reach a junction with a road. Turn LEFT. Take especial care on this very short stretch of road, as it can be busy. Soon turn LEFT along a much quieter lane.

6 Follow the lane to a staggered crossroads. Cross the main road with care and continue ahead down to Landimore. Keep on the lane; the Wales Coast Path comes in from the right after a while. At the end of the lane, go through the gate ahead onto Landimore Marsh. Keep to the track that runs ahead below Tor Gro. *Tor refers to the steep cliff behind the woodland on your left.* After about a mile, look out for a waymark post on the left. Turn LEFT here up into the wood, leaving the Coast Path.

7 Climb steeply at first and soon with a fence to the right. At the top of the wood, go through a kissing gate and follow the side of the field past gates on the right. At the end of the field turn RIGHT through a gate. Continue ahead to cross a track to a waymark post. Pass to the right of the house and head for the left hand corner of the small field. Go through a gate onto an enclosed path. At a junction of paths, keep ahead through a gate (signed to Cheriton), then through another to reach a road. Turn RIGHT and follow the road down to Cheriton and then round to the right and uphill into Llanmadoc. Keep ahead to the start, passing the Britannia Inn and the community shop and café.

1 Walk down from the crossroads into Landimore. Keep ahead until you reach a house called Tidal Reach on the left. Turn RIGHT here through a kissing gate to join the Wales Coast Path. Walk ahead to a second gate, then bear RIGHT to a third and ahead to a fourth. Now bear LEFT towards woodland through another gate and on in the same direction to join a track bearing LEFT through a gate with the woodland on the right. At the end of the wood to your right, go through a kissing gate and on to the end of the next field. Here turn RIGHT through a gate signed to Weobley Castle. Head up the left hand side of the field to a gate leading to the drive to the castle. Turn LEFT through this gate, and LEFT again to get to the castle.

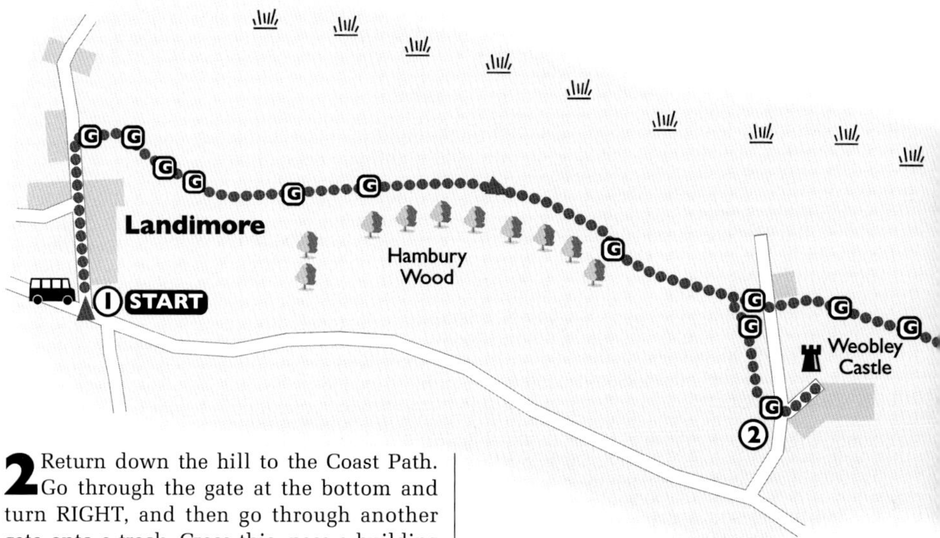

2 Return down the hill to the Coast Path. Go through the gate at the bottom and turn RIGHT, and then go through another gate onto a track. Cross this, pass a building on your left, and keep ahead, soon forking RIGHT into woodland. Cross a stile/gate, and soon turn LEFT to cross another, then immediately turn RIGHT. Go through a gate into the wood, and very soon through another. Turn LEFT here, ignoring a footpath to the right. Now go through a succession of gates (some may be open), passing a turning to Leason Wood on the right. At the end of the fields the route bends slightly RIGHT to go through a final gate, joining a stony track. Continue ahead on this, passing Stavel Hager Farm on the left.

3 Where the Coast Path bends significantly to the left by a house, leave it by forking RIGHT up a narrow path (footpath sign). Cross a stone stile into the churchyard. The church dates from the 13thC and has a number of interesting features, especially a very ancient stone slab with carvings of human and animal figures. The church is kept locked, but a key can be borrowed from the petrol station up the hill close to and clearly visible from the bus stop – see stage 4 below. Just after the church entrance there is a fascinating grave stone fastened to the wall about Robert Harry, who died in 1646; the inscription starts: 'Here lyeth my lifeles corps bereved of liveinge breath:' Walk through the churchyard to the road. Turn LEFT for refreshments; the Dolphin Inn (in a beautiful old building with low ceilings and serving real ale, also tea and coffee) is on the left and the Welcome to Town (recently renovated, and renowned for high quality food) is on the right.

4 On leaving the churchyard, turn RIGHT and walk up the steep hill for a few minutes to the main road. The bus stop for Swansea is on your left; buses going towards Llanmadoc stop on the other side of the road.

WALK 28

LANDIMORE, WEOBLEY CASTLE & LLANRHIDIAN

DESCRIPTION This is a moderate 3 mile linear walk which follows a very tranquil part of the Wales Coast Path between woodland and salt marsh – a striking contrast with the beaches and soaring cliffs on some of the other walks, and ideal if you want to get away from the more popular parts of the Gower and have a gentle stroll through pastures and woods. The walk also includes a visit to Weobley Castle, a fortified manor house dating from the 14thC, now owned by Cadw (entrance charge). Llanrhidian has an interesting old church, and two very different types of pub for refreshments. (For a longer linear walk of about 6½ miles, starting at Llanmadoc, you could do walk 27 as far as Landimore, and then start walk 28.)

START Landimore Turn bus stop (no bus stop sign) at the cross-roads (on the road between Oldwalls and Llanmadoc), SS 466928.

FINISH Llanrhidian Turn bus stop, SS 498920.

DIRECTIONS 115 and 116 buses (Mon – Sat) and 116 Gower Explorer (Summer Sundays) call at Landimore and at Llanrhidian. Parking is difficult at both places. (The same buses call at Llanmadoc, so you can easily turn this into a longer linear bus walk from Llanmadoc to Llanrhidian by doing the first 5 sections of walk 27, which will take you to the start of this walk.)

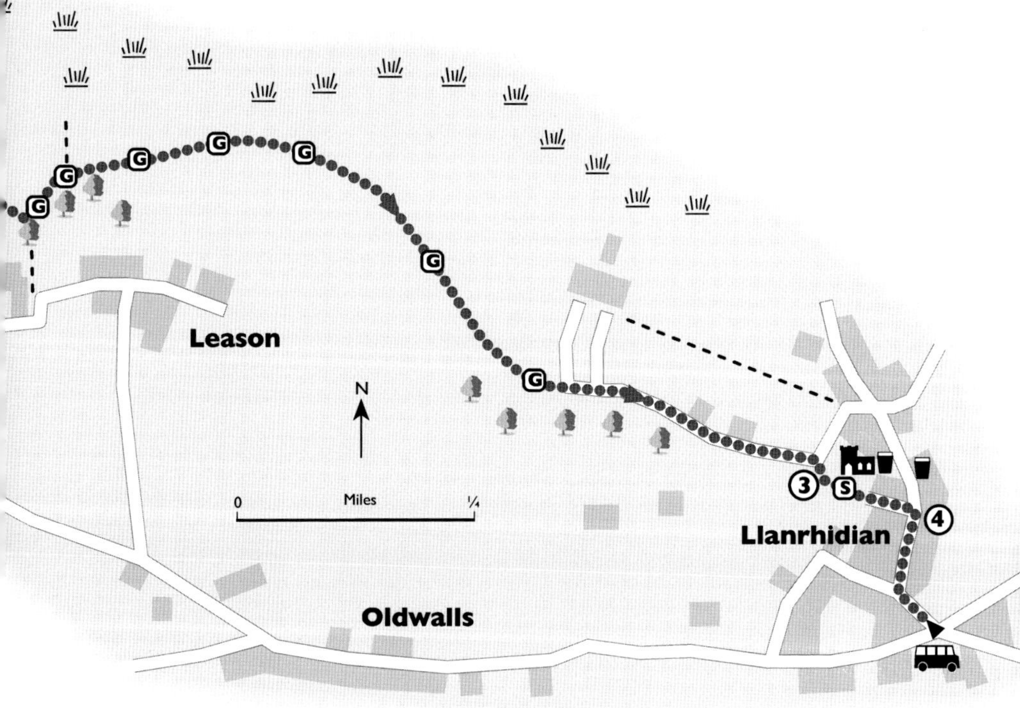

WALK 29

PARC-LE-BREOS WOODS, BROAD POOL & CEFN BRYN

DESCRIPTION This is a moderate 8 mile walk, which gives a good glimpse into the wide variety of landscapes of inland Gower, including woodland, pasture, moorland, and ridge – and also an inland pool. The longer option following section 8(B) also takes you closer to the cliffs and sea, and provides an opportunity for refreshments (summer only).

START Penmaen Church, SS 532887.

DIRECTIONS The 118 bus (Monday – Saturday) and the 118/114 Gower Explorer (Summer Sundays) between Swansea and Rhossili call at Penmaen Church. For car parking, turn right at the church, if coming from Swansea. There is a parking area just over the cattle grid on the right, and a small car park with picnic benches a little further up the lane on the left.

1 Walk up the lane with the church on your left. Cross a cattle grid and at once bear RIGHT at a National Trust pillar along a track (footpath sign). Avoid turnings to the right to houses, and fork LEFT just after Myrtle Cottage. Soon turn LEFT in front of a gate to ascend gently into woodland next to a fence. Bear RIGHT at a junction with another path coming in from the left, and when you get to a stony track, turn RIGHT. Keep along the base of the open access land until you reach a gate; turn RIGHT through this, now on the Gower Way.

2 The track soon bends to the right. Then follow the main track through the wood for about 1½ miles, until reaching a junction of tracks. Turn LEFT and soon fork LEFT, following the Gower Way waymark sign. The track eventually becomes a path, and crosses a stile out of the wood. Follow the right hand side of two fields, crossing a second stile on the way.

3 Cross a third stile and follow the path through a short stretch of woodland to reach, and cross, another stile, with a Gower Way plinth on the right. Follow the right hand side of two fields via another stile. Look for a Gower Way plinth on the right and at this point turn RIGHT onto a track.

4 Cross a shallow stream and then cross two stiles on the left. Head along the left hand side of two fields, crossing another stile. Finally another stile (no more after this!) takes you onto a track which goes to the road. Here turn LEFT, and cross over with care.

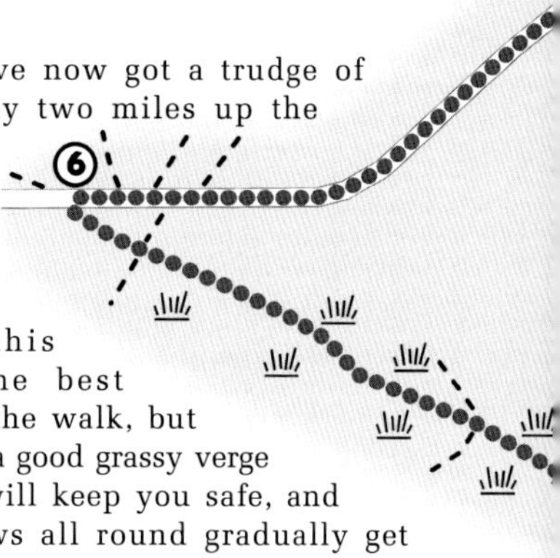

5 You've now got a trudge of nearly two miles up the road; this isn't the best part of the walk, but there is a good grassy verge which will keep you safe, and the views all round gradually get better and better as compensation for the ascent. The route also passes Broad Pool reserve, and there is a path round this if you want to have a closer look at the aquatic plants (eg water lilies) and dragonflies in summer. It's also a good spot for indigenous and migrating birds, but patience may be needed to see these.

6

6 Eventually, at the top of the ridge, you will come to a parking area on the right and bridleway signs to right and left. If you need refreshment by now, you can continue down the road to Reynoldston; continue ahead at a cross-roads to reach the King Arthur Hotel, about ½ mile from the ridge. But you will have to walk back up the hill afterwards! If you want to take the opportunity of looking at Arthur's Stone, see Section 3 of Walk 10, which reaches the road from the path to your left. Turn sharp LEFT in the direction of the sign; in less than 50 yards pass a Gower way plinth on your right. Keep

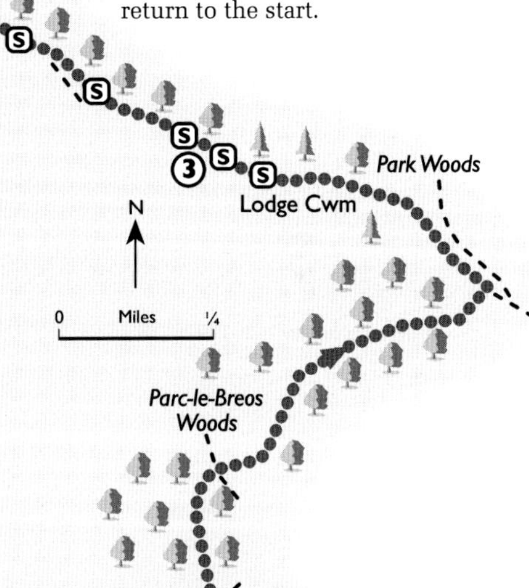

on the Gower Way past a toposcope and then in the same direction for about 2½ miles, avoiding turnings to left and right downhill. Eventually you reach Gower Way plinth 11 on the right. Here you have a choice:

7A Fork LEFT to pass a trig point on your left; about 10-15 minutes later the Gower Way turns LEFT at a plinth but you bear RIGHT and walk down to the junction with a lane. Bear LEFT to return to the start.

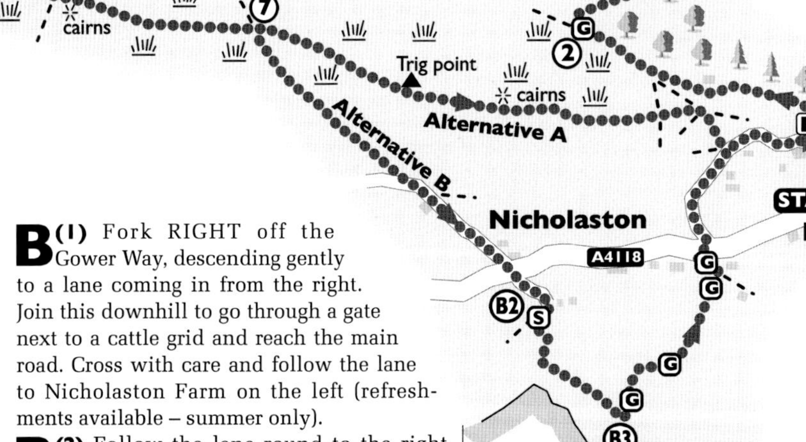

B(1) Fork RIGHT off the Gower Way, descending gently to a lane coming in from the right. Join this downhill to go through a gate next to a cattle grid and reach the main road. Cross with care and follow the lane to Nicholaston Farm on the left (refreshments available – summer only).

B(2) Follow the lane round to the right past the farm, cross a stone stile by a gate and at once bear LEFT. Keep ahead at the next junction and at a sandy patch by a large tree turn LEFT up a very steep narrow path. Ignore minor turns to left and right, but at a T junction turn LEFT (signed to Penmaen).

B(3) Pass through a gate and, later, another. Turn LEFT. Go through another gate, and turn LEFT. Soon go through a final gate to reach the main road. Turn RIGHT, cross over with care, and turn LEFT just before a bus shelter. Follow the tarmac lane, which bends gradually round to the right to return to the start.

WALK 30

PARKMILL TO THREE CROSSES - INCLUDING THREE OF THE BEST WOODLAND RESERVES

DESCRIPTION This moderate linear walk of about 6½ miles includes three of the beautiful woodland reserves owned by the Wildlife Trust of South and West Wales, two of which appear elsewhere in this book (walks 9 and 26). By way of contrast, there is also a stretch of moorland – relatively bare and bleak compared with the woods, but with its own character and beauty. The walk is very suitable for a bus walk, as there is a good bus service (Monday – Saturday) to/from the start and finish (and refreshments available at both). Allow extra time if you want to explore other paths in the reserves.

START Shepherds Store, Parkmill, SS 545892.

FINISH Bus stop next to Country Stores, Three Crosses, SS 567943.

DIRECTIONS The 118 bus (Monday – Saturday) between Swansea and Rhossili calls at Parkmill; alight at the stop for the Gower Heritage Centre (refreshments available here). If coming by car, park at the Heritage Centre, which is a short distance from the bus stop; from the entrance to the Centre don't cross the stream but walk back past houses to Shepherds store on the main road (A4118). At the end of the walk the 21B bus from Three Crosses goes to Swansea via The Black Boy at Killay, where you can change to catch a 116, 118 or 119 bus back to the Gower.

1–5 The first five sections of this walk are the same as for **Walk 9**.

6 On leaving the reserve, turn LEFT and walk up this attractive lane to emerge onto the moorland of Fairwood Common. About ½ mile further on, turn RIGHT onto a busier road, the B4271; for safety keep on the grass verge on this stretch. In about another ½ mile, turn LEFT signed to Cilonen; before long cross a cattle grid and the entrance to the reserve of Gelli-Hir Wood is on the right.

7 Now follow steps 1 and 2 of walk 26. When you get to the pond, turn LEFT past the sluice gate and continue on the path over a footbridge and uphill, bending round to the right. Eventually leave the wood over a stile. Turn RIGHT, ford a stream, pass through a gate, cross a track, and climb up through two gates and a few steps to reach a field. There is a gate at the other end of the field ahead of you, but the preferred route goes round the left hand edge of the field.

8 Once through the gate, bear LEFT to walk close to the edge of the field past a way-mark post to reach a gate. Turn LEFT through this, then turn RIGHT to join a wide track leading to the road. Turn LEFT here and cross over to go through a gate next to a cattle grid.

9 Turn RIGHT at once up a few steps and over a stile. Continue on the path through trees to reach a wider track. Turn RIGHT here and at once fork RIGHT. Follow the path round to the left, keeping close to the fence on the right. *You are now in the Crwys (Welsh for cross) Community Woodland, a small conservation site managed for biodiversity; there is a network of paths across and round it which can be explored if you have time.* Quite soon you will see a gate ahead leading to a road. Go through this and turn RIGHT.

10 At the end of the road by a footpath sign walk through a gate on the right, and continue on the path. In about 5 minutes, as the moor opens up on both sides, look for a very narrow path on your LEFT leading towards the trees. Follow this until you reach a fence; bear RIGHT to keep next to the fence to reach a stile and sign for Prior's Meadow, the third reserve on this walk.

11 Cross the stile and turn LEFT. At the first junction turn LEFT and then RIGHT at the T junction. The path now goes next to the wood to a clearing. Turn RIGHT here through a gate onto a wide track. The path crosses a number of small walkway-style footbridges. Ignore the first exit stile on the

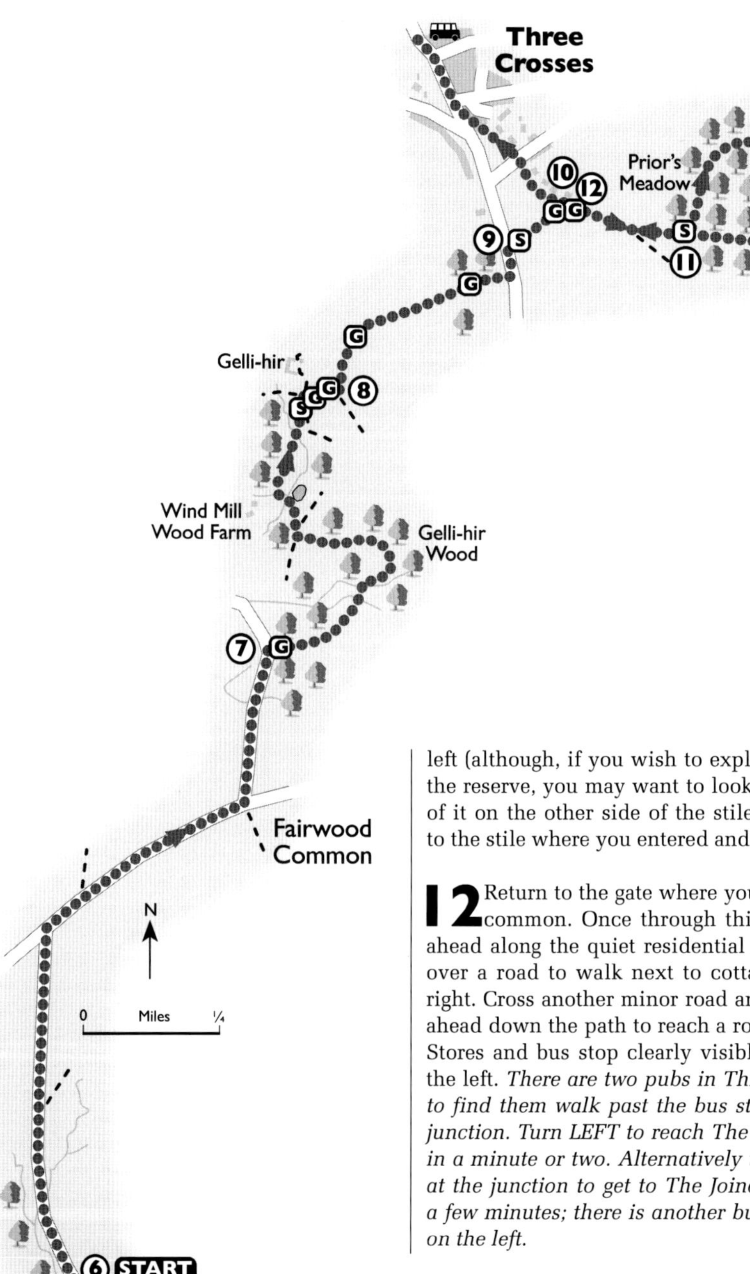

left (although, if you wish to explore more of the reserve, you may want to look at the map of it on the other side of the stile). Continue to the stile where you entered and cross it .

12 Return to the gate where you joined the common. Once through this, continue ahead along the quiet residential road. Cross over a road to walk next to cottages on the right. Cross another minor road and continue ahead down the path to reach a road with the Stores and bus stop clearly visible ahead on the left. *There are two pubs in Three Crosses; to find them walk past the bus stop to the T junction. Turn LEFT to reach The Poundffald in a minute or two. Alternatively turn RIGHT at the junction to get to The Joiners Arms in a few minutes; there is another bus stop here on the left.*

PRONUNCIATION

These basic points should help non-Welsh speakers

Welsh	English equivalent
c	always hard, as in **c**at
ch	as on the Scottish word lo**ch**
dd	as 'th' in **th**en
f	as 'f' in o**f**
ff	as 'ff' in o**ff**
g	always hard as in **g**ot
ll	no real equivalent. It is like 'th' in **th**en, but with an 'L' sound added to it, giving '**thlan**' for the pronunciation of the Welsh 'Llan'.

In Welsh the accent usually falls on the last-but-one syllable of a word.

KEY TO THE MAPS

Main road
Minor road
Walk route and direction
Walk instruction
Path
River/stream
Gate
Stile
Summit
Woods
Pub
Parking

THE COUNTRYSIDE CODE

- Be safe – plan ahead and follow any signs
- Leave gates and property as you find them
- Protect plants and animals, and take your litter home
- Keep dogs under close control
- Consider other people

Open Access
Some routes cross areas of land where walkers have the legal right of access under The CRoW Act 2000 introduced in May 2005. Access can be subject to restrictions and closure for land management or safety reasons for up to 28 days a year. Details from: www.naturalresourceswales.gov.uk.
Please respect any notices.

Published by
Kittiwake Books Limited
3 Glantwymyn Village Workshops, Glantwymyn, Machynlleth, Montgomeryshire SY20 8LY

Drawings: Morag Perrott
Cover photos: *Main* – Rhossili Bay. *Inset* – Oystermouth Castle.
Photos supplied by www.alamy.co.uk

Printed by Mixam, UK.

ISBN: **978 1 908748 38 6**